Andrew Wilson is one of my favorite w
me why. He displays a gift for weaving b
illustrations that leads me to worship G
know God's Word more deeply. And you n never look at the world the
same way.

—COLLIN HANSEN, editorial director, The Gospel
Coalition; host, *Gospelbound* podcast

Reading each chapter, I marveled anew at the kindness of God to
instruct his children with such gentle care.

—JEN WILKIN, author, *None Like Him*

Creation was always meant to point beyond itself, and Andrew Wilson
shows us the myriad and wonderful ways in which it does. This book
is packed with insight and nourishment on every page. I found myself
pointed to Christ in so many surprising and fresh ways, and provoked
to worship a God of such grace and beauty.

—SAM ALLBERRY, pastor and author

A treasure of a book from Andrew, and one that I didn't want to finish.
Seeing God through everything he has made is sheer delight.

—TERRY VIRGO, founder, *Newfrontiers*

What a wonderful book! *God of All Things* caught my attention from
the start, reminding me that all God's works—and I do mean all—
proclaim his glory. From rainbows to donkeys to everyday tools, the
things of this life really do reveal the God of life. This book is a delightful primer in learning how to truly see things for what they are.

—HANNAH ANDERSON, author, *Turning of Days:
Lessons from Nature, Season, and Spirit*

GOD OF ALL THINGS

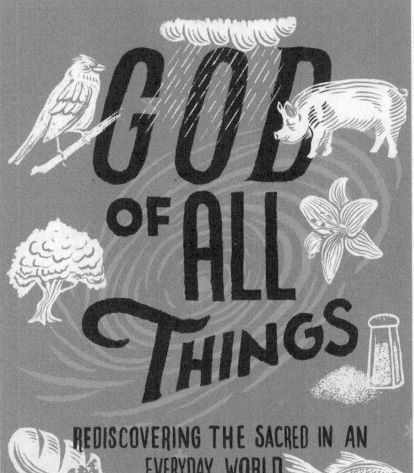

GOD OF ALL Things

REDISCOVERING THE SACRED IN AN EVERYDAY WORLD

ANDREW WILSON

ZONDERVAN
REFLECTIVE

ZONDERVAN REFLECTIVE

God of All Things
Copyright © 2021 by Andrew Wilson

Requests for information should be addressed to:
Zondervan, *3900 Sparks Dr. SE, Grand Rapids, Michigan 49546*

Zondervan titles may be purchased in bulk for educational, business, fundraising, or sales promotional use. For information, please email SpecialMarkets@Zondervan.com.

ISBN 978-0-310-10908-2 (softcover)
ISBN 978-0-310-10910-5 (audio)
ISBN 978-0-310-10909-9 (ebook)

Published in association with the literary agency of Wolgemuth & Associates, Inc.

Cover illustration and design: © *Conrad Garner*
Interior design: Denise Froehlich

Printed and bound in the UK using 100% Renewable Electricty at CPI Group (UK) Ltd

22 23 24 /CPI/ 10 9 8 7

For Andy and Janet Johnston,
who taught me how to be a pastor
and showed me how to preach from things

CONTENTS

PART 2: NEW TESTAMENT

FOREWORD

When is a building more than a building?

As I was reading the book you now hold, I found my mind returning to the church of my childhood. I spent many Sunday mornings in the sanctuary of the First United Methodist Church of Wichita Falls, Texas. Small towns in Texas are unexpected places to stumble on grandeur, but the wealthy oil barons of the early twentieth century left behind a few architectural gems. First Methodist was modeled on the design of a gothic cathedral, its soaring sanctuary wreathed in stained glass and carvings, with a massive rose window filling the chancel.

Since I am now a full-time Bible teacher, I would like to tell you I always paid rapt attention to the Sunday sermon. But the truth is my attention often wandered—to the windows, the carvings, and the items tucked into the pew rack in front of me. There, next to the hymnal and the attendance folio, was a small booklet titled "Eye Gate: Sermons in Symbols," written by Eleanor M. Robbins. The booklet was filled with explanations of the images that surrounded me in glass and stone and wood, each carefully chosen to teach a truth about God.

So while I often failed to listen carefully to the sermon, I nevertheless learned that the peaked windows and arches of the sanctuary were meant to resemble hands folded in prayer. I learned that the seven steps from the nave to the altar symbolized the seven attributes of the Lamb written in Revelation 5. The rose window contained six doves to represent the gifts of the Spirit prophesied in Isaiah 11:1–2. There were pomegranates and lilies, stars and flames, thorns and chalices and clovers, each image or item echoing a biblical truth. The light fixtures were designed to look like censers, representing the prayers of the saints rising to God. Worked into the front of the pulpit was an intertwined monogram of the Greek letters alpha and omega. The entire building was preaching the Word of God in symbol, all without uttering a word.

When is a rose window more than a rose window?

In the tradition of the medieval gothic architects of Europe, the architects of First United Methodist Church constructed a building not just to dazzle the eyes but also to teach. Deliberately and masterfully, they designed a space that repeated the words of Scripture in memorable ways through stone and glass and wood. Any passing visitor to the church, Christian or not, would be moved to wonder by the beauty of the space they had designed. But those who recognized its symbols would be moved to worship and remembrance.

The Bible, too, is the work of an architect, though we sometimes forget this. Through the pens of human authors, that divine architect has filled our sacred text with carefully chosen imagery. Many readers have remarked on the Bible's poetry or its historical narratives, but those with an eye for its imagery will be moved to worship and remembrance. Each of the authors of the sixty-six books of the Bible shares something in common with those cathedral builders: a commitment to teach through repetition what is true about God in memorable ways.

When is a mountain more than a mountain? When is a garden more than a garden?

We live in a time when our education systems often fail to teach us how to properly read literature—with an eye for authorial intent. We approach a book assuming that it is our job to assign it meaning, asking, "What does this book mean *to me*?" But the work of the reader, properly understood, is not to assign their own personal meaning to a text but to uncover the meaning the author intended to convey. No author sits down to write without first considering how and what they wish to communicate—the architectural design behind what they are writing. No author puts pen to paper or fingers to keyboard without first asking, "How can I help my reader arrive at a proper understanding of my message?"

If we lack a discerning eye, one carefully attuned to the author's intent, we arrive at the text disadvantaged. And this is especially tragic when we are reading the most important literature ever penned—the Word of God. We read its words and come away with a plain meaning or a personal meaning, but we miss the deeper meaning. We are like a casual visitor to the cathedral, awed by its architectural grandeur, but unaware of the symbols the architect has carefully chosen to draw us in to worship and remembrance. Our eyes are untrained. We fail to see as we ought.

This book is an "eye gate." When is a mountain more than a mountain? When are gardens, trees, wind, animals, or even musical instruments more than the objects themselves? When they are intended to draw us deeper into understanding, when the one who created them uses them to teach those he loves. The Bible's literary architecture far surpasses the splendor of any cathedral. It employs consistent themes and images chiseled across sixty-six books by forty different authors spanning 1500 years. The resulting work is nothing short of staggering and worthy of a lifetime of study. Learning its layered language draws us more deeply into worship. And its words and images are not a secret formula or a magic decoder ring for understanding the Bible. They are simple learning tools, employed deliberately and given graciously to us by God, that the words of his book might settle deeply into our souls.

Knowing that the citizens of Wichita Falls, Texas, might never visit the grand gothic cathedrals of Europe, Eleanor M. Robbins lovingly preserved their architectural legacy for a new generation of the faithful. In *God of All Things*, Andrew Wilson has done much the same for you. Here is an invitation to see what generations of believers before us saw, to enter the sacred space of the Scriptures and lift up our eyes. Reading each chapter, I marveled anew at the kindness of God to instruct his children with such gentle care. Lovingly and eloquently, Andrew unfolds for us the blueprints, and gestures to the details. He extends to us an invitation to worship and to remember, and to receive the benediction for all whom the Spirit enlivens: "Blessed are your eyes, for they see."

—JEN WILKIN, AUTHOR AND BIBLE TEACHER

INTRODUCTION

THE THINGS OF GOD

O Lord, how manifold are your works!
In wisdom have you made them all;
the earth is full of your creatures.
—PSALM 104:24

God didn't have to create a material world. He could have made an entirely spiritual universe, with no matter or physical laws. He could have made the angels and quit while he was ahead. He could have decided to make nothing at all and carry on rejoicing in the fellowship of the Trinity for all eternity.

But instead he made a universe filled with things. Objects. Stuff. Planets, weather, colors, animals, vegetables, minerals. People, complete with noses and kidneys and bodily fluids. It is curious: an immaterial and entirely spiritual God created a thoroughly material and physical world. Perhaps it should surprise us more than it does.

INTRODUCTION

So why did God make *things*? Have you ever wondered that? You're reading Scripture and enjoying its spirituality when suddenly there's an extended section on hair or locusts or water. It jolts. You are struck by the strange physicality of the text. Somehow it feels as though material like this ought not to be in the Bible. So why is it?

We could answer that question a number of ways. One is to picture God like a fountain, bubbling up with so much joy that it overflows into the creation of the world.[1] God does not create because he has to or because he lacks anything. He creates because his delight in being God is so abundant and bountiful that it spills out into a universe of wonders.

Another is to see the physical world as a display case of God's multicolored wisdom. This is the explanation in Psalm 104, one of Scripture's most beautiful songs. God's marvelous intelligence and creativity become visible to us in the things he has made. The psalmist, without access to encyclopedias or the internet, already had a whole bunch of examples in mind: valleys, lions, storks, wine, rock badgers, oil. The more of creation we discover—tropical fish, triceratops, Iguazu Falls, wallabies, coffee—the more our amazement of God's wisdom increases. "O LORD, how manifold are your works! In wisdom have you made them all; the earth is full of your creatures" (Ps. 104:24).

Created things teach us practical wisdom as well. Ants show us the power of diligence, even if we feel small or insignificant: "Go to the ant, O sluggard; consider her ways, and be wise" (Prov. 6:6). We can learn about sexual fidelity from hot coals, about making money from the flight of eagles, about handling anger from churning butter (Prov. 6:27–29; 23:4–5; 30:33). The growth of a tiny mustard seed into a huge bush is an illustration of the power of faith (Matt. 17:20). Jesus' teaching is full of things—sheep, birds, flowers, coins, seeds, trees, fields, salt, light, feet, rain, the sunrise—which instruct us how to live, simply by being there. Watch and learn.

For Paul in Romans 1, creation reveals God's invisible power and divine nature. Few of us can stand in front of the Grand Canyon or see a high-definition picture of the Horsehead Nebula without wanting to praise somebody or something for the majesty of what is before us. Some of us will suppress that urge. But those of us who don't and allow the song of gratitude to swell within us like a storm will find ourselves concluding all sorts of things about our Maker. The God of the Sahara must be vast, boundless, and expansive. The God of quarks must have an unimaginable eye for detail. The God of wombats must have a sense of humor. Everything in creation has theological implications, and one of the joys of being human is figuring out what they are.

What all of these answers have in common is the fact that creation points beyond itself. Things exist not for their own sakes but to draw us back to God. In Augustine's image, the gifts of God in creation are like a boat which takes us back to our homeland: a means of transport which we can (and should) celebrate but never mistake for the destination itself.[2] C. S. Lewis talks about following the sunbeams back to the sun so that we enjoy not just the object of goodness but the source of good.[3] Creation preaches to us. The things of God reveal the God of things.

Sometimes we look at things upside down on this point. Theologians point out (rightly) that the language used for God in Scripture is often anthropomorphic, and we should not take it literally. (God does not literally have a mighty arm, the nations are not literally under his feet, sacrifices do not literally reach his nostrils, and so on.) But this is only half the story, and in some ways the less important half.

It might be more helpful to say that the world is theomorphic: things take the form they do because they are created to reveal God. We describe God as "the Rock" not just because rocks exist and they provide a good picture of safety and stability. Rocks exist because God is the Rock: the Rock of our salvation, the Rock who provides water in the desert, the Rock whose work is perfect and all his ways are just. When we flip things around like this, we get a very different picture of the purpose of creation, of physical stuff, of things. Ever since the beginning, the surface of this planet has been covered with rocks, and every one of them has been preaching a message of the faithfulness, security, and steadfastness of God. "For their rock is not as our Rock; our enemies are by themselves" (Deut. 32:31).

This book is an attempt to listen to messages like that. Some chapters offer an exposition of creation, a meditation on who God is, as revealed through specific things. Others consider what a particular thing represents in Scripture and ask what we can learn from it. Others do a bit of both. As you read them, my hope is that you will get a deeper understanding not just of Scripture but of the world you live in, and ultimately of the God who made it all. (I love the idea that you might be walking down the street one day, see one of the things that we consider in this book, and get jolted out of your daydream into wonder and worship.) The book asks questions like, What does the existence of honey tell us about God or about what he has done in Jesus Christ? What are we supposed to learn from the fact that he created pigs, flowers, donkeys, fruit, and earthquakes? Might there even be significance in things that human beings have made: pots, trumpets, tools, cities? After all, "the earth is the Lord's, and everything in it" (Ps. 24:1 NIV).

Come and see.

PART 1

OLD
TESTAMENT

1

DUST

THE IMAGE OF GOD

*Then the L*ORD *God formed the man of dust from
the ground and breathed into his nostrils the breath
of life, and the man became a living creature.*

—GENESIS 2:7

Dust goes unnoticed, for the most part. It surrounds us all the
time, but unless we work in construction, we hardly ever
see it. When we do, it is usually because we are trying to get rid
of it: hoovering, dusting, sweeping, cleaning behind the fridge,
or whatever. I notice it when we first turn the heating on each
winter, because everyone starts sneezing. I notice it when the
children touch the television screen, leaving a small handprint

of black in a sea of a gray powder. I notice it when I go into a shed, lift up a sheet or tarpaulin, and watch the shafts of sunlight illuminate a cloud of fine particles which rise, billow, dance, and eventually settle. Otherwise, although I am continually touching and breathing a cocktail of hairs, pollens, fibers, soil, mites, and skin cells, I try not to think about it.

Dust speaks to us of decay. It comes about through the decomposition of other things, whether animal, vegetable, or mineral. Dust in a home tells us that our cells have died recently. On a building site, it tells us that something has been knocked down or destroyed. When it dominates the landscape, it tells us that plants cannot grow here because the soil is too shallow or the rain too infrequent. Ghost towns and postapocalyptic movies are covered in it, highlighting the loss not just of creatures or structures but of civilization itself. When the greens and browns of life have been and gone, we get the beige of death.

And God says to us, you are made of that.

It doesn't sound very encouraging. Dust evokes decay, decomposition, and death, in Scripture as much as for us, which means that at least part of what it is to be dust people is that we will one day be dead people. When humanity falls, choosing the tree of the knowledge of good and evil ahead of the tree of life, the curse upon us—"for you are dust, and to dust you shall return" (Gen. 3:19)—is clearly a reference to mortality. In a world where people pursue the elixir of life as enthusiastically as ever, whether in the form of cryogenics, transhumanism, genome editing, or any other death-denying fad, the Bible makes the certainty of dying as clear as it can be: "It is appointed for man to die once, and after that comes judgment" (Heb. 9:27). We came from the soil, and one day we will again be part of it.

People sometimes talk as if Christians believe in immortality and secular materialists don't. The reality is almost the opposite. The certainty of death is integral to Christianity—our future revolves around not immortality but resurrection—while those most eager to postpone or even escape death are usually those with no resurrection hope whatsoever. Early churches met in catacombs, surrounded by corpses. To this day, churches have graveyards and are filled with memorials and crypts for the faithful dead. Our message centers on the one who died and was raised, not someone who carried on living indefinitely in suspended animation. Our sacraments are graphically morbid: we bury people in water, eat a broken body, and drink blood. So as the rich world spends good money trying to avoid (or at least to avoid thinking about) death, part of the mission of the church is to remind them of the obvious. Earth to earth, ashes to ashes, dust to dust.

Surprisingly, though, the first time we are described as being created from dust, it has nothing to do with death. It has to do with life. "Then the LORD God formed the man of dust from the ground and breathed into his nostrils the breath of life, and the man became a living creature" (Gen. 2:7). Humans have not sinned at this point. The tree of life is still available to us. Yet the writer insists that we are created from the dust of the ground. What does this mean?

Partly, it is a way of saying that we are part of the physical creation: we are made of matter, of stuff. We are created to bear the image of God, who is spiritual and invisible, so it is important that we have tangible bodies that occupy space. We are not angels or disembodied spirits; we are built from atoms and molecules, carbon and oxygen.

But it is also a way of highlighting our supernatural, God-breathed origins. In some of the Egyptian and Akkadian creation stories, humans are described as made out of clay, which you can kind of imagine: most of us, with a bit of practice, could form clay into something that looks pretty much like a person. But you could never do that with dust. The most complex shape I could make out of dust would be a pile, and even then it would be instantly scattered by a gust of wind. What causes a bunch of particles to come together into a human being is not any property inherent in the bunch of particles; it is nothing less than the breath of the Lord, which animates the dust and causes it to become a living soul. Without the breath of God, we are nothing more than a pile on the floor. With it, we are bearers of the divine image.

That very realistic description of a human—the dust of the ground plus the breath of the Lord, physical and spiritual, body and soul—is actually a source of great comfort in Scripture. For good theological reasons, a Christian understanding of humanity places a strong emphasis on the image of God, and the essential dignity and grandeur that it confers to all people. We are kings, priests, ambassadors, rulers, made for a little while lower than the angels and crowned with glory and honor (Ps. 8:5), and that has crucial implications for the way we treat one another.

But alongside that (vital) emphasis on dignity, there is also an appropriate humility that comes from remembering that "I . . . am but dust and ashes" (Gen. 18:27) and that "he knows our frame; he remembers that we are dust" (Ps. 103:14). Knowing that we come from the ground keeps us grounded; the Latin word *humus*, which means "soil" or "earth," gives us the words humility and human.[4] And there is such reassurance in knowing that God, in his compassion and fatherly kindness, sees us not only as princes, expected to rule the world, but also as dust and ashes, expected to fail sometimes and cry out for rescue. As Hannah sang so beautifully, one of his favorite hobbies is lifting people from the dust and ashes—marginal, broken, poor, and needy people like her, and indeed like me—and seating us with the princes (1 Sam. 2:8).

We are dust, and to dust we shall return. We may find it liberating, unsettling, or terrifying, but it is true nonetheless: one day the cells that compose us will be swirling in the autumn leaves, wedged between sofa cushions, and hidden behind radiators. The same is true of all the world's most powerful and influential people. As with Ozymandias in Shelley's famous poem, their apparently invincible empires will finally turn to dust. So will we.

But only for a while. Ultimately, as Daniel saw, "those who sleep in the dust of the earth shall awake, some to everlasting life, and some to shame and everlasting contempt" (Dan. 12:2). Dry bones in a death valley will be filled with divine breath and raised to life (Ezek. 37:1–12). In Adam we are all dust people, and we decompose accordingly, but in Christ we then rise to become heavenly people for whom dust and decay, mortality and corruptibility, are things of the past. Paul, describing the resurrection to people who couldn't quite believe it, explains that "just as we have borne the image of the man of dust, we shall also bear the image of the man of heaven" (1 Cor. 15:49). Our future, Paul says, will be modeled not on the man who came out of the soil but on the man who came out of the tomb.

So get all your hoovering done now. The new creation will be dust free.

EARTHQUAKES

THE GLORY OF GOD

*Now Mount Sinai was wrapped in smoke because
the L*ORD *had descended on it in fire. The smoke of
it went up like the smoke of a kiln, and the whole
mountain trembled greatly.*

—EXODUS 19:18

Appearances of God are often accompanied by earthquakes.
Mountains tremble. The rocks split. People quiver in fear,
building foundations rattle, and the land rumbles. When the
earth is visited by its King, it shakes. Why?

The most frightening example is probably the first one,
when God descends on Mount Sinai in fire. Moses has done

his best to prepare the Israelites, but they are nonetheless terrified when, on the morning of the third day, the apparently ordinary mountain beside which they are camping appears to be on fire, shrouded in smoke, covered in a thick cloud out of which thunder and lightning are issuing forth and, with a deafening trumpet blast, getting louder and louder. "The whole mountain trembled greatly" (Ex. 19:18). So did the Israelites (v. 16); they were so frightened that despite having just been promised that they were God's treasured possession and were destined to be kings and priests on earth, they stood far away in terror, refused to approach God, and insisted that Moses speak to him instead (20:18–19). The writer wants us to see the connection, so he uses the same word (*charad*) for the quaking of the earth and the quivering of the people. As the psalmist would write many centuries later, the glory of the Lord makes the people tremble and the earth quake (Ps. 99:1). Earthquakes are associated with the fear of God.

The exodus generation, however, is notoriously forgetful. A while later, a group of the people who were at Sinai that day decide that Moses is too big for his boots and challenge his leadership. "Why . . . do you exalt [yourself] above the assembly of the LORD?" (Num. 16:3). Moses responds with a simple test: if you guys all die a natural death, then that will prove that I haven't been sent by God, but if the earth suddenly splits open and swallows you up, then it will show that you have despised the Lord (vv. 28–30). We know this is not going to end well. Sure enough, "as soon as he had finished speaking all these words, the ground under them split apart. And the earth opened its mouth and swallowed them up" (vv. 31–32). This is not just an Old Testament thing; there is a very similar sequence in the last book of Scripture, where a massive earthquake splits the world, and the rulers of the earth ask the mountains and rocks to fall on them and hide them from the wrath of the Lamb (Rev. 6:12–17). Earthquakes are associated with the judgment of God.

In several passages, they also represent divine speech. As Ezekiel is commissioned for his prophetic ministry to Judah, he hears "the voice of a great earthquake: 'Blessed be the glory of the LORD from its place!'" (Ezek. 3:12). Psalm 29, perhaps the richest meditation on the voice of God in the entire Bible, describes it as thunderous, powerful, majestic, and glorious and then compares it to an earthquake: "The voice of the LORD shakes the wilderness; the LORD shakes the wilderness of Kadesh" (Ps. 29:8). If we were describing it today, we might compare God's voice to the noise of an airplane breaking the sound barrier, or a rocket launch: a thunderous, booming, awe-inspiring roar which drowns out all other noise with its voluminous authority. When God speaks in Scripture, he sounds like thunder, like an earthquake, like a rushing wind or a mighty waterfall, which is why it is so surprising when Elijah hears God speak not in a hurricane or an earthquake or a fire but in a gentle whisper (1 Kings 19:11–13). Earthquakes are associated with the voice of God.

So far, so obvious. You can see why the shaking of the earth would make people scared and make them think of divine judgment, and why it would be used to illustrate the power of God's word. But I think earthquakes represent something deeper than that, something which stands behind the fear, the judgment, and the mighty voice. Earthquakes are associated with the glory of God.

You can see the link in a number of texts. When the seraphim make their magnificent proclamation of divine glory—"Holy, holy, holy is the LORD of hosts; the whole earth is full of his glory!" (Isa. 6:3)—the temple shakes to its very foundations. When Haggai describes the filling of the temple with glory, it is accompanied by an international earthquake (Hag. 2:7). The psalms connect the glory of God and the shaking of the earth (Ps. 97:4–6; 104:31–32). Again, it is worth asking: why?

To answer, we need to know what the Hebrews meant by "glory." If you hear the word glory in English, the chances are that you think of triumph, beauty, and splendor, which is what the Romans meant by *gloria*. But the Hebrew word for glory, *chabod*, was slightly different. It derived from the word for heavy or weighty, a connection which Paul makes when he talks about the "eternal weight of glory beyond all comparison" (2 Cor. 4:17). Glory, in a sense, is heaviness. Gravitas. So when the ark of God was captured by the Philistines, this was described as the "glory" (*chabod*) departing from Israel, and then immediately afterward we hear that the hand of God was "heavy" (*chabed*) upon the Philistines, afflicting them with tumors and breaking their gods in pieces. To speak of God's glory, in biblical terms, is not just to speak of his splendor and beauty (though that too) but also to speak of how weighty, heavy, and substantial he is.

Now consider: what happens when something glorious, heavy, and weighty descends upon something lighter, flimsier, and less substantial? Displacement. The heavy thing shunts the lighter thing to one side, and the lighter thing has to move—or quake or even tremble—to make space for the heavy thing, whether it wants to or not. If I jump into a pool, I cause a small waterquake. If I drop a giant block of gold onto a frozen pond, I cause an icequake. The weighty substance displaces the flimsy one, and the flimsy one shakes, gives way, and is forced to reorient itself around the weight of glory.

So what happens when the glory of God, the divine *chabod*, descends upon Mount Sinai or the Jerusalem temple or anywhere on earth? An earthquake. God displaces that which is trivial and ephemeral, and forces the earth to reorient itself around him. The earth trembles and quivers in response to the arrival of a far more glorious and substantial reality. The Lord reigns! Let the peoples tremble! Let the earth quake!

The same thing happens when God descends upon people. It is not just that Mount Sinai trembles, as we have seen; the people of Israel do as well. It is not just the temple that shakes in Isaiah's vision; Isaiah himself is undone by the *chabod* and cries out, "Woe is me! For I am lost" (Isa. 6:5). When people encounter the true God, they experience a selfquake. That's one way you can tell if you've met Israel's God or simply a figment of your imagination. A made-up God will leave your world undisturbed, conveniently aligning with your priorities without displacing anything, because ultimately you are more glorious than it is. The real God, however, will land in the middle of your life like an elephant crashing through the ceiling, displacing your sin, changing all your priorities, and forcing you to reorient yourself around the weight of glory.

Yet earthquakes are also associated with the gospel of God. The two most important and hope-filled events in the history of the world, the crucifixion and resurrection of Jesus, were both accompanied by earthquakes. When the King of the earth died, the earth shook and the rocks split (Matt. 27:51). When he rose on the morning of the third day, the same thing happened again (28:2). Both earthquakes prompted fear in those who were there, and in different ways manifested the judgment, the voice, and the glory of God. But they showed more than that. They showed that the Lord was not just greater and weightier and more glorious than the earth, or than the self, but more substantial than the two mightiest and fiercest enemies we have: sin and death. The Prince of Glory died and caused a sinquake. The King of Glory rose and caused a deathquake. The heavy depths of the unshakable Savior crashed into the lightweight shallows of the enemy and displaced him forever, along with all of his minions.

When the King of the earth descends, everything on earth—the people, the mountains, the temple, the principalities and powers, even death itself—is shaken. "Therefore let us be grateful for receiving a kingdom that cannot be shaken, and thus let us offer to God acceptable worship, with reverence and awe" (Heb. 12:28).

CHAPTER
3

PIGS

THE WELCOME OF GOD

> *"The pig, though it has a divided hoof, does not chew the cud; it is unclean for you. You must not eat their meat or touch their carcasses; they are unclean for you."*
>
> **—LEVITICUS 11:7–8 NIV**

I like to call it the pig paradox. On the one hand, no animal is dirtier, smellier, or uglier than a pig. The unfortunate combination of snouts and snorts makes them deeply unattractive. They roll around in mud and eat their own feces. They have become a byword for mess ("her room is a pigsty"), infidelity ("he is such a pig"), ignorance ("pearls before swine"), disaster ("a pig's ear of it"), overeating ("greedy as a pig"), and unappealing facial features ("pig-nosed," "piggy-eyed"). When they are clustered together, you can smell them from miles away; I once had a night's sleep in Yorkshire ruined by the stench from a nearby hog farm. More than a billion people avoid eating or touching them, on religious grounds, considering them filthy and untouchable. You can see why.

On the other hand, they taste sensational. Pork belly, pancetta, honey-glazed gammon, prosciutto, nduja sausage, crackling, ham, barbecued ribs, salami, trotters, hog roast: it is hard to believe that such a wide range of cuts and flavors could come from the same animal. And that is before mentioning the smell of sizzling bacon, which is surely the most delicious aroma there is (with apologies to coffee, fresh bread, and baked cookies). Bizarrely, if you were to create a smell spectrum, from the vilest stench to the most enticing aroma, pigs would find themselves at both ends of it, depending on whether it was before or after they died. How can something that smells so bad when it is alive smell so great when it isn't? How can death transform something from filthy and untouchable to aromatic and delightful? Hold that thought for a moment.

Pigs, under the law of Moses, were off-limits to Israel. Both Leviticus and Deuteronomy command that they are not to be eaten or touched, and although various reasons have been suggested for this (their smell, their habits, the danger of eating them uncooked), the reason given in the law is simply that they have divided hoofs, have cloven feet, and do not chew the cud. It can look a bit arbitrary to us, but God simply declares that some animals are clean and some animals aren't: cows, sheep, pigeons, goats, and scaly fish are fine, but camels, shellfish, snakes, birds of prey, and animals with paws are not.[5] And the most detestable of unclean animals—the ones Isaiah mentions to show just how depraved people can be, even to the point of eating swine flesh (Isa. 65:4; 66:17)—are pigs. As gentiles, by nature unclean and separated from Israel ourselves, we can feel a certain sympathy for them.

That is not where the similarity between pigs and gentiles stops. The first person who ever preached the gospel to gentiles was the apostle Peter, and he did so only because he saw a vision of a sheet full of unclean animals (Acts 10:9–16)—a vision in which, we may assume, pigs played a starring role—and heard a voice telling him to eat them, since "what God has made clean, do not call common" (v. 15). Non-Jewish people like me got baptized only because Peter saw a bunch of pigs and other unclean animals, and then saw a bunch of gentiles, and then saw the resemblance. "You yourselves know how unlawful it is for a Jew to associate with or to visit anyone of another nation," he explained to the gentiles who had invited him over for a visit, "but God has shown me that I should not call any person common or unclean" (v. 28). That's a nice way of putting it. Even Peter, not always the most diplomatic of the apostles, had the good manners not to mention that his hosts were the equivalent of a sheet full of pigs, scallops, and snakes.

The result of that vision was extraordinary. By the end of Acts 10, the first ever handful of gentiles had been baptized in water and filled with the Spirit and were speaking in tongues and praising God (vv. 44–48). Now there are upward of two billion of us: formerly unclean, cloven-footed, cud-chewing gentiles who have been washed from our dirt and purified from our sins and now offer ourselves as fragrant offerings to the God who makes common things clean. It is the pig paradox again. Death—in our case, the death of Christ—has taken that which was filthy and untouchable, and made us aromatic and delightful by the grace of God.

The most famous pig-related incident in Scripture is the moment when Jesus delivers a demon-oppressed man, only to send the demons into a herd of two thousand pigs, who all promptly charge down a cliff and drown in the sea. You can read it in Mark 5:1–20, and it's just as bizarre as it sounds. Generations of interpreters, seeking to make sense of a baffling story, have found all kinds of tenuous principles in the passage, such as one person is worth more than two thousand pigs, you should always ask a demon's name before casting it out, and so on.

But when we bear in mind what pigs and gentiles have in common in Jewish thought, we start to see ourselves in this poor, broken, demonized man. He is unclean, impure, an outsider, surrounded by pigs, and unable to access the presence or the people of God. As gentiles, so were we. He lives among the tombs, with death all around him, naked and ashamed, without hope and without God. So did we. He is oppressed by the powers of darkness, crying out in pain and harming himself, beyond the reach of any human power. So were we.

Then he meets Jesus. The Savior not only sets him free from the devil's tyranny but humiliates his enemies (and ours) by driving them, and all the uncleanness and impurity they represent, down the cliff and into the sea. The man is restored to his right mind and clothed in new garments. He is visibly transformed by the encounter, such that those who have known him before come to fear the power of Jesus. He is desperate to follow his new Master and Savior. As the story closes, he is given a new mission:

to return to his community and "tell them how much the Lord has done for you, and how he has had mercy on you" (Mark 5:19). The pigs have died, but in their death the man has found new life and has been thoroughly delivered from the powers that oppressed him and the uncleanness that tainted him. So have we. Like the prodigal son, we stumble toward our father, desperate for more than pig pods and reeking of swine, and we are as surprised as anyone when he hugs us, kisses us, and dresses us in a fresh set of clothes before inviting us in to a feast.

In Christ, pigs become bacon. It's the welcome of God. Those whom you wouldn't have wanted in the garden, for all their stinking and snorting and snuffling, experience death and find themselves welcomed into the kitchen for everybody to savor. Stench dies, impurity is washed away, and we who were once unclean become a pleasing, crispy, tasty, aromatic offering to God. Therefore "what God has made clean, do not call common" (Acts 10:15).

LIVESTOCK

THE SUBSTITUTION OF GOD

> *One bull from the herd, one ram, one male lamb*
> *a year old, for a burnt offering; one male goat*
> *for a sin offering; and for the sacrifice of peace*
> *offerings, two oxen, five rams, five male goats, and*
> *five male lambs a year old. This was the offering*
> *of Nahshon the son of Amminadab.*
>
> **–NUMBERS 7:15–17**

One of the strangest things about Scripture, for a modern reader, is the amount of time it spends talking about farm animals.

Many of us have had a similar experience. We are new to Christianity, and the day comes when we get hold of a Bible and start to read it from the beginning. We are excited by what it may contain: ancient wisdom, life-changing insights, the words of life, the presence of God, or whatever it is. It opens well. The world is created, flooded, and scattered. We meet a family whose characters are compelling and whose ups and downs mirror our own. We see God rescue them from slavery. The first seventy chapters or so move from epic to soap opera to adventure story, and with the occasional exception (looking at you, Genesis 36), it's a gripping read.

But then something weird happens. No sooner have we finished the Ten Commandments than we notice that the writer's interests have apparently changed. Instead of a rollercoaster narrative, we have long speeches about tents and priests, clothes and rituals. Unexpected and grimace-inducing phrases start appearing, like "the fat that covers the entrails" or "the long lobe of the liver." We thought we were in a story about marriages, betrayals, miracles, and escapes; now it's about bulls, lambs, rams, and goats. Farm animals become major characters, dominating what is usually considered the Bible's most boring book (Leviticus), as well as what is undoubtedly its most boring chapter (Numbers 7). Without warning, an epic tale of global events and human relationships has morphed into a book about livestock.

At one level, our surprise should not be a surprise. Few things express the difference between modern and ancient lifestyles more than our relationship with animals, so we might expect to find the Israelites talking about livestock more than we do. Most of us are not farmers or ranchers. We get food and drink from the shop, buy clothes made of cotton or polyester, power our machines with electricity, store our money in banks, and get around using planes, trains, and automobiles. In the ancient Near East, by contrast, people relied on livestock for meat, milk, eggs, clothes, shoes, power, plowing, milling, traveling, and going into battle. Flocks and herds were the primary marker of wealth in many cultures (hence the connection between the words capital, chattel, and cattle). Nearly everybody would interact with farm animals on a daily basis. If you go back to Genesis with that in mind, you'll see them in virtually every chapter, being created, named, killed, eaten, traded, milked, yoked, argued about, stolen, and in one case used as a somewhat improbable disguise. Livestock were the stock of life, so they pop up everywhere.

Even so, none of this gets to the root of why farm animals feature so prominently in Scripture. It is true, and hopefully interesting, but it misses the point. The main way in which the Bible talks about livestock is in the context not of wealth or work but of worship. Farm animals are substitutes.

Not always in a good way. Sometimes they function as substitutes for God: as idols, as physical representations of divinity, as objects of worship in themselves. This never ends well. The famous example is when the Israelites have just escaped slavery and ask Aaron to build them a golden calf, which they promptly worship as if it had taken them out of Egypt, and they face severe consequences. (Aaron's response, on being confronted about this by his brother Moses, wins the award for the worst excuse in Scripture: "I threw [the gold] into the fire, and out came this calf" [Ex. 32:24].) The less famous example sees Israel worshiping goat demons (Lev. 17:7), which leads to a clarification of the laws about sacrifice. Israel was certainly not unique here; many civilizations worshiped idols in the form of bulls, goats, or rams, including the Egyptian society from which they had just been rescued. Clearly, there was something about the strength and life-giving fertility of farm animals which made ancient people want to worship them.

More positively, however, they also substituted for people. In the most common sacrifice, the *qorban olah* (usually translated "burnt offering" or "ascension offering"), the bull, ram, or goat functioned as a substitute for the individual Israelite in their journey of worship toward God. It was presented by the worshiper from their own flock or herd—a costly step in itself, given how valuable such animals were—to be inspected by the priest, who would check that the animal was without blemish. The worshiper would lay their hand on its head, identifying the animal as their representative, and kill it. Next the priest would manipulate its blood in various ways before burning the entire corpse, with the animal ascending in smoke to heaven "as a pleasing aroma to the Lord." In some offerings, the worshiper would then eat a fellowship meal before God, being careful to eat only the animal's flesh, as opposed to its blood (representing its life) or its fat (representing the best portion, which belonged to God). Finally, the priest would bless the worshiper.

The symbolism of the *qorban olah* (Leviticus 1) revolved around worship, not forgiveness. It wasn't a sin offering. The point of it was not to atone for sins but to experience fellowship with God. The animal was identified with the Israelite, so as the smoke ascended to heaven, it was as if the worshiper were rising too, entering the presence of God and then enjoying a fellowship meal with him. Human beings could not ascend to God's throne on their own terms, so they needed a substitute—a bull, a goat, or a ram—to ascend on their behalf in smoke and fire. The aim of the offering was union with God.

Livestock also substituted for sins. In a number of ceremonies, most publicly on the Day of Atonement (Leviticus 16),
livestock carried the transgressions of the people. On the tenth
day of the seventh month, the high priest would put two goats
in front of the Lord and cast lots over them. He would kill one
of them as a sin offering, to make atonement for the Holy Place.
Then he would lay his hands on the other one's head, confess
the sins of the people, and send it out into the wilderness. With
this heavily symbolic double whammy, Israel would see the two
aspects of their forgiveness acted out in front of them: the cleansing of their sins through the blood of one goat, and the removal
of their sins through the exile of the other. It showed them that
their transgressions were not just dead but removed.

I remember my friend Graham Marsh illustrating this using
two balloons. Imagine these helium balloons represent your sins,
he said. One of them—here he took a knife and stabbed the
balloon—is burst, demonstrating that everything you have done
wrong has been defeated with a bang. The other—and at this
point he opened the fire doors at the back of the auditorium and
let go of the balloon—is released, rising higher and higher into
the sky, until it is so far away you can no longer see it. That's
how the substitutionary goats work on the Day of Atonement, he
explained, and that's how the substitutionary sacrifice of Christ
works for you. Your sins have been destroyed, and you have been
cleansed from them. But they have also been taken away from
you, so far that you cannot even see them, as far as the east is
from the west.

Farm animals are substitutes. They might be sinfully fash-
ioned as replacements for God, like a golden calf or a bull's head.
They might represent people in worship, like a ram rising as a

smoky offering into the presence of God. They might take the consequences of sins upon themselves, like the two goats on the Day of Atonement.

But they are imperfect substitutes. They cannot measure up to the reality they represent. They don't offer themselves willingly; they have to be sacrificed over and over again, day after day, year after year, giving us a regular reminder of how sinful we are; and although they can cleanse us externally and ritually, they cannot cleanse us internally as well, making us perfectly holy and releasing our consciences forever. For these reasons, "it is impossible for the blood of bulls and goats to take away sins" (Heb. 10:4). Livestock always fall short.

Except the Lamb. There is one farm animal who is worshiped not just by a handful of idolatrous Israelites but by every tribe and tongue and people and nation (Rev. 7:9–10). There is one farm animal who offers himself so willingly, sheds his blood so unreservedly, and ascends to God so permanently that he is able to take billions of people with him, straight into the presence of God. There is one farm animal whose substitutionary offering for sin is so perfect that it can save anyone, cleanse the conscience, and last forever. In Genesis, a ram substituted for one young man (Gen. 22:13). In Exodus, a lamb substituted for each family (Ex. 12:3). In Leviticus, a goat substituted for the nation (Leviticus 16). In the gospel, a Lamb substituted for the entire human race.

"Behold, the Lamb of God, who takes away the sin of the world!" (John 1:29).

TOOLS

THE WEAPONS OF GOD

*Jael the wife of Heber took a tent peg, and took
a hammer in her hand. Then she went softly to
him and drove the peg into his temple until it
went down into the ground while he was lying fast
asleep from weariness. So he died.*

—JUDGES 4:21

In the first battle of Armageddon, the enemy commander was killed with camping equipment.

Speculation about the next one has been the stuff of bestselling books and blockbuster movies. There is talk of a world government, flying locust-scorpion warships, bar codes, conspiracies, the

EU, nuclear weapons, and a giant meteor steaming toward earth with Bruce Willis on board. But the first time a war was fought at the Valley of Megiddo—later known as *Har-Magedon*—the decisive blow was struck with the most everyday objects imaginable. Sisera, commander of the mighty Canaanite armies, had his head crushed by Jael, a tent-dwelling woman, using a mallet and a tent peg (Judg. 4:17–22).

It's a striking story in all kinds of ways. A woman is judging Israel at the time, which is unusual in itself: Deborah, whose name means "bee" and who stings her enemies to provide honey for her friends. The man charged with leading the Israelite army, Barak ("lightning"), refuses to fight unless she goes with him. Israel wins the battle despite overwhelming odds. When the victory is celebrated in song, the main characters are (again) three women: Deborah, described as "a mother in Israel"; the mallet-wielding Jael; and Sisera's luridly vile mother, who is looking forward to hearing the details of how her son captured "a womb or two for every man" (5:30). The peg through the temple is also pretty unforgettable.

Yet this story also forms part of a wider pattern that appears repeatedly in Scripture, a pattern in which Israel defeats her enemies with tools instead of weapons. In this case, Israel has no shields or spears but conquers instead with a peg and a "workmen's mallet" (5:8, 26). In the previous story, Shamgar defeats the Philistines with a cattle prod (3:31). In the next one, Gideon wins with jars and trumpets (7:19–23). In the one after that, a citizen of Thebez kills Abimelech with a millstone thrown from a tower (9:53), the second time in six chapters that an obscure woman has crushed the head of a powerful man with a domestic implement. Jericho's walls were brought down by a musical instrument. Israel was liberated from Egypt, and then Amalek, with a staff which would otherwise be used for steering sheep. God, it seems, likes power tools.

But why? What is going on here? I suspect at least three things.

The most obvious one is that Israel is being reminded, over and over again, that her military security is grounded not in her strength, numbers, weaponry, or ability but in the power and faithfulness of the God she worships. In several cases, Israel doesn't have any weapons because her enemies have forbidden her from making them; God's people are so inferior in military terms that they cannot even make a sword, far less raise an army. So they have no option but to fight with whatever tools they have available—pitchforks, flour grinders, camping gear—and trust the Lord to fight on their behalf.

In that sense the victory of tools over weapons is a subset of a larger biblical pattern, in which strong armies who worship false gods are overcome by weak armies who worship the true God. The very strangeness of the weapon is the whole point; nobody could win with *that* unless God was with them. It could be a tent peg or a cattle prod. It could be an angel. It could be a jawbone or a pebble or a song or an altar soaked in water that suddenly catches fire. Sometimes it's an apparently natural phenomenon, like a storm at Megiddo or a thunderclap at Ebenezer. Whatever the means of victory, it rams home the point that Israel's success comes not from the strength of her army but from the strength of her God. "Not by might, nor by power, but by my Spirit, says the LORD of hosts" (Zech. 4:6).

There is also a hopeful, eschatological contrast here. The triumph of tools over weapons, work over warfare, is itself a prophetic statement of the peace that God will ultimately bring to the world. Mallets and millstones defeat shields and chariots because, in the end, the world will be filled with farmers and millers rather than generals and armies. The future, as Isaiah saw, is one in which the trappings of war are superfluous. Swords will become plowshares, and spears will turn into pruning hooks. "Every boot of the tramping warrior in battle tumult and every garment rolled in blood will be burned as fuel for the fire. For to us a child is born, to us a son is given, and the government shall be upon his shoulder" (Isa. 9:5–6).

One day, the cosmic war which we have all been fighting since the garden will be over. All of Christ's enemies will be under his feet. On that day, there will be no need for shields or warheads. But there will be plenty of need for tent pegs and millstones, rods and staffs, cattle prods and musical instruments. Swords and spears will be obsolete, so they will get hammered into plowshares and pruning hooks instead, at which point we will use them to plow the fields and prune the vineyards of God's new world, turning grain and grapes into bread and wine.

The richest contrast between the two, however, is hinted at in one of the Bible's most cryptic passages. Zechariah sees a vision of four horns and is told that the horns represent a military threat to God's people. (This is also what they represent in the book of Daniel and in Revelation.) He then sees four craftsmen and hears that although the nations will try to scatter Israel, the craftsmen will terrify them and cast them down (Zech. 1:18–21). On its own, it is a bizarre, puzzling image, as are most of Zechariah's night visions. But when seen in the broader context of Scripture, it points to a beautiful fulfillment. The enemies of God will come like armies brandishing horns, and the people of

God will come like craftsmen brandishing tools, and the people of God will conquer.

The fulfillment of this vision comes at the cross. Rome, the most powerful military force the world has yet seen, gathers a battalion of soldiers to inspect Israel's king. They are armed; he is stripped. They come with swords and spears; he comes in nothing but the name of the Lord God. They are horns; he is a craftsman. They carry the most advanced weapons available. He is carrying the ordinary carpenter's tools he grew up with: nails, hammers, and planks of wood.

Yet when the dust of battle settles, the warriors are no match for the carpenter. The craftsman casts down the horns. The tools overpower the weapons. And the head of the enemy is crushed, right through the temple.

CHAPTER

6

HORNS

THE SALVATION OF GOD

Hannah prayed and said,
"My heart exults in the LORD;
my horn is exalted in the LORD.
My mouth derides my enemies,
because I rejoice in your salvation."

—1 SAMUEL 2:1

Many women have had the experience of praying for a child. If the request is not granted, it can be a source of immense pain and sorrow. If it is granted, it often results in joyful celebration and thanksgiving. Scripture gives us a number of examples: Eve highlighting the promise of God, Sarah laughing, Leah hoping that her fertility will make her husband love her, Rachel exclaiming that her shame has been taken away, Elizabeth keeping quiet for the first twenty weeks, and a young woman who (famously) rejoices in her pregnancy despite *not* having prayed for a child or even having had sex in the first place. Those of us who have prayed for children may be able to relate to each of these responses and perhaps imagine ourselves reacting in a similar way if our prayers were answered. But one thing that none of us would do, I suspect, is to do what Hannah did and sing a song about horns.

"My heart exults in the LORD; my horn is exalted in the LORD" (1 Sam. 2:1). Hannah has just had a miracle baby; what have horns got to do with it? Are we talking about musical instruments, animal headgear, or something else entirely? And why? Then, as Hannah finishes her prayer, she returns to the horn theme. "The LORD will judge the ends of the earth; he will give strength to his king and exalt the horn of his anointed" (2:10). The word appears in the first and last lines of her thanksgiving prayer for Samuel, and it pops up again when Zechariah gives thanks for the birth of John the Baptist (Luke 1:69), as well as in numerous psalms. Seriously, what have horns got to do with babies?

In most cases, not much. We named our son Samuel because of this very story and give thanks to God for him every day, but to my knowledge we have never talked about horns in doing so. But Hannah's boy Samuel, and Zechariah and Elizabeth's boy John, are not like most other children. They both grow up to be prophets: prophets who prepare the way for, preach about, and then anoint the long-awaited king of Israel. Samuel is the forerunner of David, the chosen and beloved king who will rule in place of the corrupt ruler (Saul), save God's people from her enemies (the Philistines), and slay the giant who is taunting her (Goliath). John is the forerunner of Jesus, the chosen and beloved King who will rule in place of the corrupt ruler (Herod), save God's people from her enemy (sin), and slay the giant who is taunting her (death).

So Hannah's song is not a personal meditation in the delivery room, a sort of Bronze Age "Isn't She Lovely." It's more like "The Star-Spangled Banner." It is a shout for joy on the battlefield, celebrating the fact that "the bows of the mighty are broken, . . . the feeble bind on strength . . . [and] the adversaries of the Lord shall be broken to pieces" (1 Sam. 2:4, 10). That's why she sings about horns.

The horns of an animal, first and foremost, are a sign of strength. They are fundamentally weapons, used for fighting off predators, defending offspring, or competing with other members of the same species for land, supremacy in the hierarchy, or the right to mate with a particular female. Battles between horned animals can be fierce, the stuff of nature documentaries and viral YouTube videos. A pair of male impalas can fight to the death. When two bison face off, the impact shakes the ground. A buffalo, armed with nothing but a pair of horns, can gore and defeat the most powerful predator in the world (google "lion vs. buffalo"; some of the footage is sensational). So horns represent strength, power, and victory in battle. We still use the symbolism today in the names and logos of our sports teams: rams, buffaloes, bulls, rhinos, even Vikings. (Having said that, I should note that teams represented by horns or horned animals have a dismal Super Bowl record of 1–10, so it may not be such a good strategy.)

This is what the psalmists are getting at when they say that "the LORD is . . . the horn of my salvation" (Ps. 18:2) or "the horns of the righteous shall be lifted up" (75:10) or "[God] has raised up a horn for his people" (148:14) or "his horn is exalted in honor" (112:9). A fight between two horned animals often begins with both males lifting up their horns as high as possible in preparation for battle, much as warriors might draw their swords or cock their rifles. To describe God as raising a horn for his people, in that context, is to say that God is the one who fights for us. The power to overcome is his, not ours. In many cases, biblical characters said this from personal experience, having just seen God rout his enemies with a flood, an ambush, a stick, or an orchestra or give his people supernatural power to prevail against a vastly superior opponent. "He trains my hands for war, so that my arms can bend a bow of bronze" (18:34).

In the ancient Mediterranean world, the horn also represented plenty. There is debate as to why—it is probably a combination of the horn's strength, the use of the image in Greek mythology, and the way a horn resembles a strange fusion of the human reproductive organs—but it was frequently used to represent fertility and abundance. This found its most famous expression in the image of the cornucopia, a giant horn-shaped container full of fruit, vegetables, flowers, and nuts (and rather different produce in Suzanne Collins's *The Hunger Games*). Although there is no explicit reference to the horn of plenty in Scripture, there may be an equivalent in the basket of firstfruits that Israel presented as an offering, or the basket of summer fruits that Amos saw centuries later (Deut. 26:2; Amos 8:1–2).

Now combine those two symbolic meanings into a third. Imagine a horn filled with victorious strength and abundant plenty on the head of a mighty beast about to prevail in battle, and then imagine the horn being broken off, turned upside down, filled with oil, and poured all over the head of Israel's king. Picture the horn of anointing, which covers the individual with a sticky liquid representing power and strength, blessing and fullness, and marking him off from his peers as Mr. Royal Oil.[6] This is not a dab on the forehead. It is not the sort of thing you could apply respectably and secretly, as they did at the queen's coronation in 1953. It would be incredibly obvious, cascading off the king's head onto his shoulders, staining his clothes, and making his face shine. It would leave no doubt that this person had been smeared, anointed, with the power and abundance of Israel's God and indeed with his very Spirit. "Then Samuel took the horn of oil and anointed him in the midst of his brothers. And the Spirit of the LORD rushed upon David from that day forward" (1 Sam. 16:13).

That is the image we draw on whenever we refer to Jesus as the Messiah. (The Hebrew word *mashach* means to "smear" or "anoint.") It's the picture we evoke when we use the word Christ or when we refer to ourselves as Christians. This can be easy to forget in a world where many people think Christ is simply Jesus' surname, but it is the claim we are making nonetheless: that Jesus is the one over whom the horn of God's strength has been lifted high, in whom the riches of God's fullness are found, and upon whom the oil of God's Spirit has been poured. In him we find the power, plenty, and person of God himself, fighting our battles, providing for our needs, and shining with the Holy Spirit's presence. In him we find the victory of God in human form, the most potent weapon anywhere and the only one we need to save us from our enemies. Zechariah was right: "[The

Lord] has raised up a horn of salvation for us in the house of his servant David" (Luke 1:69).

Horns represent victorious strength and fertile abundance and the royal oil of God's Spirit. (That's without mentioning the horns of the altar, which would require another chapter, or the horn as a musical instrument, which we cover in our section on trumpets.) Like so many biblical symbols, they point us to Jesus, God's perfect expression of each, which is ultimately what Hannah was rejoicing about that day, and why a thousand years later both Mary and Zechariah riffed off her song when they had babies of their own.

But now that we've seen Jesus in that light, it is tempting to go right back to the beginning of Scripture, to the first time horns are mentioned, and wonder whether Jesus is there too. Abraham, on the verge of killing Isaac, looks around and sees a ram "caught in a thicket by his horns. And Abraham went and took the ram and offered it up as a burnt offering instead of his son" (Gen. 22:13). Like Jesus, the horn of our salvation, this ram has been imbued with great power. But his strength is precisely what leads him to be caught, to be crowned with thorns from a thicket, and to be set forth by God on Mount Moriah as a substitutionary sacrifice for others.

The first few times I read Hannah's prayer, I couldn't understand why she was singing about horns. But now, praise God, her song has become mine: "My heart exults in the LORD; my horn is exalted in the LORD. My mouth derides my enemies, because I rejoice in your salvation. . . . The LORD will judge the ends of the earth; he will give strength to his king and exalt the horn of his anointed" (1 Sam. 2:1, 10).

GALAXIES

THE GREATNESS OF GOD

"Is not God high in the heavens?
See the highest stars, how lofty they are!"

–JOB 22:12

In the middle of the constellation of Scorpius, there is a large star that looks red when you see it with the naked eye. Its color prompted the Greeks to call it Antares, "rival to Mars," and by most counts it is the fifteenth-brightest star in the night sky. You may have seen it. (More accurately, you may have seen it as it was before Columbus discovered America. Antares is 550 light-years away, so if it disappeared today, we would be approaching the end of the twenty-sixth century before anyone realized.) It is one of around two hundred and fifty billion stars in the Milky Way, our local galaxy (if you are happy to use the word local for something that takes light a thousand centuries to cross).

Galaxies are beyond our understanding. As soon as we use words like billion, light-year, or parsec, we are talking about the unimaginable. The statements I have just made are true, as far as we know, but I cannot even make sense of them myself; the human mind is not really designed for thinking at that scale. That is why, when the Scriptures want to cut the legs out from under human arrogance, they often just point to the night sky, ask who created it, and let the magnitude of the galaxies speak for itself.

I find it difficult to fathom the size of the earth, let alone anything larger. It weighs around six million million billion tons. It is so big that it seems flat when you're standing on it, even though it is spherical. The earth's crust, which feels pretty huge to me—from the heights of Mount Everest to the depths of the Mariana Trench—is so thin relative to the rest of the planet that it is the equivalent of a postage stamp stuck on a soccer ball. You can see the power of God's questions to Job: "Where were you when I laid the foundation of the earth? Tell me, if you have understanding. Who determined its measurements—surely you know! Or who stretched the line upon it?" (Job 38:4–5).

Yet in planetary terms, the earth isn't large at all. It is a fraction of the size of Saturn and smaller than Jupiter's Great Red Spot (fig. 1). David had no way of knowing this, but he marveled that the God who furnished the solar system had any idea who he was. "When I look at your heavens, the work of your fingers, the moon and the stars, which you have set in place, what is man that you are mindful of him, and the son of man that you care for him?" (Ps. 8:3–4). Quite.

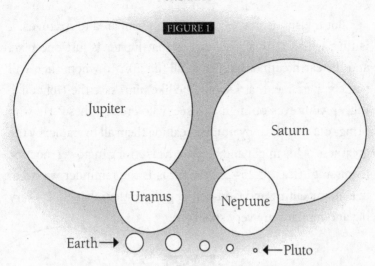

FIGURE 1

Jupiter, however, is only one-thousandth the size of the sun. If the earth were the size of a pea, Jupiter would be a grapefruit, and the sun would be a giant beach ball, capable of holding 1.3 million earths inside it and weighing 99.8 percent of the entire solar system (fig. 2). Every second, the sun loses six million tons of its mass—equivalent to one million African bull elephants—yet it doesn't even make a dent.

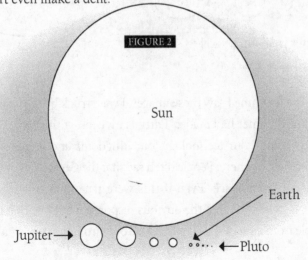

FIGURE 2

47

But the sun is not a very big star. Compared to Arcturus, it is tiny, which at this scale means that Jupiter is just one pixel and the earth cannot be seen at all (fig. 3). "To whom then will you compare me, that I should be like him? says the Holy One. Lift up your eyes on high and see: who created these? He who brings out their host by number, calling them all by name; by the greatness of his might and because he is strong in power, not one is missing" (Isa. 40:25–26). Arcturus is the reminder we need, in a man-exalting and God-denying generation, that God is very big and humans are very small.

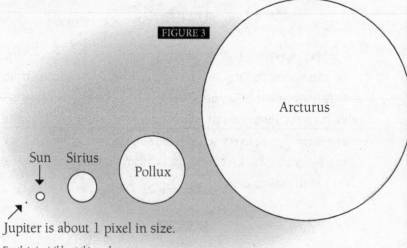

FIGURE 3

Arcturus

Sun   Sirius

Pollux

Jupiter is about 1 pixel in size.

Earth is invisible at this scale.

The first time I saw these images, I was struck by the comment that the designer had made: "Earth is invisible at this scale." None of our boasts, our technology, our kingdoms and achievements can be seen out here. People often say that the Great Wall of China is visible from space. Even if this were true (which it basically isn't), it strikes me that the obvious response would be that it isn't visible from *most* of space; it is visible only from the very small and specific bit of space directly above the Great Wall of China. Fifty years ago John Lennon boasted that the Beatles were bigger than Jesus; a generation later Oasis asked when God had last played Knebworth. But then the camera tracks back to reveal Arcturus, and it all sounds rather silly. "Is not God high in the heavens? See the highest stars, how lofty they are!" (Job 22:12).

Then we see Antares.

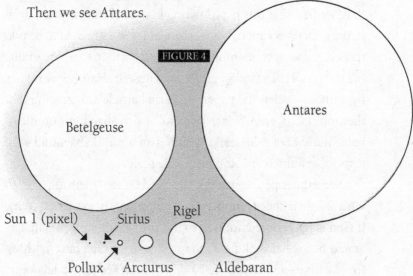

Jupiter is invisible at this scale.

Now Arcturus looks like a pea, the sun is just one pixel, and Jupiter is invisible (fig. 4). Antares is so vast that we don't even know how big it is, but if it were placed at the center of the solar system, it would reach to somewhere between the orbits of Mars and Jupiter. (It's not even the biggest star up there; VY Canis Majoris is thirty times larger again, which amounts to a staggering three billion times the size of the sun, but you have to stop somewhere.) Most of us have never heard of Antares, but it will be up there quite happily tonight, offering a permanent and resounding challenge to God shrinkers in every generation, who assure us that the Lord could never say this, know that, or do the other. Oh yes he can, says Antares. Oh yes he can, says Jeremiah. "Ah, Lord God! It is you who have made the heavens and the earth by your great power and by your outstretched arm! Nothing is too hard for you" (Jer. 32:17).

All of this is without leaving the Milky Way. Once we do that, we find that this breathtaking festival of stars is just a drop in the galactic ocean, in which there are now estimated to be two trillion galaxies, containing even more stars than there are grains of sand on all the world's beaches and deserts. Hardly a year goes by without a scientific paper or journal article announcing that the universe is even bigger than we had realized: an unimaginable number of galaxies, containing an unthinkable number of stars, of genuinely incomprehensible scale.

Sometimes people wonder why God created them all, or even whether their sheer number casts doubt on his existence. Why, if God is really so committed to the people who bear his image, would he bother making so many galaxies which have nothing to do with us and which we could not even see until a few years ago? I can think of all sorts of answers to that: to humble us, to express his boundless creativity, to inspire us to worship, to give us a taste of the infinite, to help us understand phrases like "far more abundantly than all that we ask or think" (Eph. 3:20) and "unsearchable riches" (v. 8), or simply to give him the joy of making them all. But occasionally I wonder whether he did it for the fun of seeing our jaws fall open when we read Genesis 1:16 (NIV): "He also made the stars."

STONES

THE TRIUMPH OF GOD

> *The stone that the builders rejected*
> *has become the cornerstone.*
> *This is the LORD's doing;*
> *it is marvelous in our eyes.*
>
> **—PSALM 118:22–23**

On the night before he died, Jesus sang a hymn with his friends (Matt. 26:30). It was just after the Lord's Supper and just before he went to the Mount of Olives to pray. We cannot be certain, but in all likelihood the hymn was taken from Psalms 113–118, the "Hallel psalms," which were (and still are) traditionally sung by Jews at Passover. He may have sung all of them.

He may have sung just the last one, a celebration of God's rescue from distress, enemies, and the threat of death. Either way, it is beautiful to think that the last thing Jesus did before walking to the place of his capture was to sing a song of deliverance. "The Lord is on my side; I will not fear. What can man do to me? . . . I was pushed hard, so that I was falling, but the Lord helped me. . . . I shall not die, but I shall live, and recount the deeds of the Lord" (Ps. 118:6, 13, 17). But the most dramatic moment in the psalm comes toward the end. "The stone that the builders rejected has become the cornerstone" (v. 22). You can imagine the twelve of them singing into the clear April night, even though only one of them truly grasps the implications. "This is the Lord's doing; it is marvelous in our eyes" (v. 23).

It seems odd that at such a pivotal moment in world history, Jesus would sing about stones. It seems even odder when you realize that this is not a one-off. Five days earlier, immediately after entering Jerusalem, Jesus had quoted this same passage as the punch line of his parable about wicked tenants (Matt. 21:42). In Hebrew, the punch line involves a provocative pun: a story about a rejected son (ben) becomes a lyric about a rejected stone ('eben), which then becomes the most foundational stone of all. For those with ears to hear, it is a parable about Jesus: the Son, and the Stone, who is cast aside, only to be vindicated and exalted to the place of highest honor.

Raising the stakes, Jesus then brings two further Old Testament passages about stones into the conversation. "And the one who falls on this stone will be broken to pieces," he says cryptically, "and when it falls on anyone, it will crush him" (v. 44). This is now a baffling fusion of images. The first quotation is taken from Isaiah 8:14–15, a prophecy of judgment in which the stone is the LORD himself: a rock of stumbling, a pebble in the shoe that will trip up many in Israel and cause them to fall. In the second, taken from Daniel 2:34–35, the stone is the kingdom of God, which, though it looks small and unimpressive to begin with, ends up smashing every worldly empire and filling the entire earth. So now we have three Old Testament stones, which all appear to be representing different things.

More remarkable still, Jesus is claiming to be all three of them. In Daniel's terms, he is the little stone that crushes idolatrous empires and whose rule eventually fills the world. In Isaiah's image, he is the Lord in person, who will be a source of offense to Israel and cause many to stumble and fall. He is also the stone the psalmist sang about, first rejected and then turned into the cornerstone. This is the story of his life in three stones. God comes to earth, offends people, challenges worldly powers, gets rejected both by his people and by the empires of the world, and is then lifted up to become the foundation of God's temple and is given a kingdom that fills the earth. No wonder he finished the Lord's Supper by singing about it.

In our world, some of these connections are more obscure. In Jesus' world, the giant stones with which the temple was built were made of the same stuff as the things you might stub your toe on while walking down the street. But we don't really talk about stumbling stones and cornerstones. We talk about pebbles or bits of gravel, and we put them in a different category than we put the things that solidify buildings, like concrete foundations or iron girders. We miss the linguistic connection and often miss the point as well.

So it might be helpful to think about mangoes. In the center of every mango is a stone, about two inches long. The stone is as hard as granite: if you bite into a ripe mango without knowing it is there, you can seriously damage your teeth. It is also fiendishly difficult to remove. Because mangoes are so delicious, there are dozens of YouTube videos out there on how to get rid of the stone and make the whole mango look like a hedgehog. (YouTube lies. In my experience the method never works, and the one in the video doesn't look remotely like a hedgehog anyway.) But although we treat the stone as a nuisance, disrupting us from enjoying the sweet taste of ripe fruit, it is ultimately the most important part of the mango. It is the seed, the life giver, the foundation for all future generations of mango trees. It is a stone of offense and a rock of stumbling, which most of us remove and throw away, but having been cast out, it becomes the cornerstone and fills the world with fruit.

If you step back from the final week of Jesus' life and consider how stones function in the Scriptures as a whole, you begin to notice the wide range of things they signify. For one thing, stones seal things. They cover wells to stop animals from falling in (Gen. 29:2–3). They block entrances and exits to stop people (or even lions) from getting in or out (Dan. 6:17). They are the security doors of the ancient world.

Stones build things. They build houses and altars and temples. The sheer size of the stones in the Jerusalem temple, some of which still sit there today, was a source of amazement and admiration to the disciples. "Look, Teacher, what wonderful stones and what wonderful buildings!" (Mark 13:1). Although Jesus was less impressed—"There will not be left here one stone upon another" (v. 2)—this was not because he didn't care about God's house being built with stones; it was because the stones he was going to use would be alive (1 Peter 2:5).

Stones memorialize things. When Jacob woke up from his vision of a ladder reaching from heaven to earth, he named the place Beth-El, "house of God," and marked the spot with the stone he had slept on, turning his pillow into a pillar (Gen. 28:18–19). Joshua commemorated the crossing of the Jordan with a heap of twelve stones at Gilgal (Josh. 4:20). After leading Israel to victory against the Philistines, Samuel raised a "stone of help," an 'eben-ezer, so that the Israelites would not forget that "till now the Lord has helped us" (1 Sam. 7:12). When subsequent generations wonder whether God is among them or has ever helped his people, the stones cry out.

Stones are used for judgment. Several times in Scripture you find a heap of stones being raised over a person who has been judged by God, like Achan (Josh. 7:26), the king of Ai (8:29), or Absalom (2 Sam. 18:17). On other occasions, as horrible as it is to think about, stones are used to execute people for certain crimes. This explains why hailstorms serve to enact divine judgment, as they do from Exodus to Revelation: "The Lord threw down large stones from heaven on them as far as Azekah" (Josh. 10:11). It shows why it matters that Goliath, who had publicly blasphemed the living God, should be killed with a stone rather than a sword, javelin, or spear (1 Sam. 17:49). It also forms the backdrop to one of Jesus' most famous statements, that only the person without sin should throw the first stone (John 8:7).

Yet the most famous stone in history—more foundational than the temple walls, more marveled at than Stonehenge—is the stone that wasn't there. The stone in front of Jesus' tomb was meant to be a seal, a security door, preventing anyone from getting in or out. (Russell Moore describes Matthew 27:65, Pilate's instruction to the soldiers at the end of Good Friday, as the most hilarious line in the Bible: "Go, make it as secure as you can." Good luck with that.) It ended up becoming the foundation stone on which the new world will be built. It is the *'eben-ezer* that reminds all generations just how far the Lord has helped them. It has executed judgment on death itself. It is the stone which was thrown to one side by the only one who was truly without sin.

As the sun rose that morning, the unmovable stone of death was rejected so that the Stone of Life whom the builders rejected might become the Cornerstone. This, as Jesus and his disciples had sung three nights before, was the LORD's doing. And it is marvelous in our eyes.

HONEY

THE SWEETNESS OF GOD

My son, eat honey, for it is good,
and the drippings of the honeycomb are sweet
to your taste.

—PROVERBS 24:13

Breakfast cupboards are a fairly recent invention. When my eyes run along the shelf immediately above my toaster, I am faced with a whole range of options that would have been unknown to people a few hundred years ago. Jams, jellies, marmalades, preserves, and fruit curds require so much sugar that they were practically impossible until sugarcane started being produced commercially. The same is true of chocolate spread.

Marmite wasn't eaten anywhere until the twentieth century, and in most parts of the world it still isn't (since plenty of people are convinced that it is the closest equivalent to what evil tastes like, I don't see that changing anytime soon). Bovril was invented in 1870. Modern breakfast cereals began twenty years before that. So the only two things on my breakfast shelf that would have been recognized by George Washington or Napoleon are oats (and I have no idea who in my family actually eats those, although I have my suspicions) and the richest, sweetest item in the cupboard: honey.

Honey is astonishing. If I were to share a potluck meal with Shakespeare, Genghis Khan, Muhammad, Cleopatra, Queen Esther, Tutankhamun, and Abraham, we would be baffled or disgusted by many of the contributions, but we would all come together over the golden jar in the middle. Honey lasts through the centuries, not just metaphorically but literally; it never goes out of date, so if an enterprising archaeologist were to find a sealed pot of Stone Age honey in a cave somewhere, you would be able to spread it on your muffin for tea. And both of these things are true because of the truly remarkable thing about it: honey is unprocessed. In our world, virtually everything we eat is treated, sterilized, cooked, or pasteurized and then combined with other things to make it more palatable. (If you've ever tried cutting all sugar or salt out of your diet, you'll know how difficult it is to live without them.) But honey is almost unique in having no need for additives, flavorings, or preservatives. It is luxuriously sweet and delicious without even trying.

We have bees to thank for that. They rummage around inside flowers to find nectar, sometimes collecting honeydew as well, and digest it as they fly. On returning, the foragers perform a dance which explains to the others where they have found the nectar—a dance which, unthinkably, factors in the position of the sun relative to the food source, the distance they have flown, the quality of the food available, and even the speed of the wind—and pass the nectar on to their colleagues in the hive, who pass it around from bee to bee until it is digested enough to be stored. This takes up to twenty minutes. When it is ready, they put it in the cells of the honeycomb and gradually raise its sugar content by evaporating the water, using the heat of their bodies and continually flapping their wings to keep the air circulating. When the sugar level is high enough to ensure that the honey won't ferment, they seal the cell with wax and move on to the next one. As far as I know, nobody has ever published an academic paper proving the existence of God from the existence of bees, but someone probably should.

The result of this foraging, dancing, digesting, storing, heating, flapping, and waxing extravaganza is an amber-colored, viscous liquid as sweet as granulated sugar. It is sticky, rich, golden, and delicious. It brightens the eyes and enlivens the soul (1 Sam. 14:27–29). That is why we use it as a complimentary term for words (honeyed), smells (honeysuckle), and voices (mellifluous) and as an affectionate term for people we love ("Hi, honey"). It is also why we share our enjoyment of it with Samson, racoons, skunks, the Egyptian pharaohs, honey badgers, Solomon, and Winnie-the-Pooh. "My son, eat honey, for it is good, and the drippings of the honeycomb are sweet to your taste" (Prov. 24:13).

And God is the honey maker. A God with no stomach, no tongue, no sweet tooth, and no need for calories came up with the properties of honey before he created atoms. He invented its color and its texture, imagined the way it would seep into the holes of crumpets, and pictured the indescribable flavors that would result when it was mixed with sea salt and turned into ice cream. He conceived of its spreadability, longevity, and medicinal properties. He foresaw the elaborate dance of the bees and smiled. Then he spoke it all into being, and behold, it was good.

Scripture never talks about divine sweetness or uses honey as an illustration of God. It would be so easily misunderstood: it would fuel our tendency to domesticate God and imagine him as a comfortable addition to our cozy lives, a flavoring we can opt for according to our mood, a spiritual condiment. (A glance at the contemporary church suggests we don't need any more encouragement in that direction!) Yet honey appears sixty times in the Bible, and in most cases it represents one of three things. Each of them reveals something of what, if we were not careful, we might call the sweetness of God.

Honey represents God's land and God's rescue. If we read the story of the burning bush in Exodus 3, most of us focus (rightly) on those glorious three expressions of the divine name: "the God of Abraham, . . . Isaac, and . . . Jacob" (v. 6), "I AM WHO I AM" (v. 14), and "the LORD" (v. 15). But the promise Moses receives that day, and which he later relays to the Israelites, is this: "I have come down to deliver them out of the hand of the Egyptians and to bring them up out of that land to a good and broad land, a land flowing with milk and honey" (v. 8; see also v. 17). This is a beautifully poetic way of describing redemption from captivity into freedom. Israel has known slavery and bondage, but the Lord is rescuing her into sweetness and abundance. She has eaten bitter herbs, but she will eat milk and honey. That promise is at the heart of the Old Testament story, which is why it is repeated so often (Ex. 13:5; 33:3; Lev. 20:24; Num. 13:27; 14:8; Deut. 6:3;

11:9; 26:9, 15; 27:3; 31:20; Josh. 5:6; Jer. 11:5; 32:22; Ezek. 20:6, 15). And it is one of the most common biblical ways of describing God's commitment to bless and rescue his people. When our circumstances are dire, we still worship a God who takes the vinegar of our situation and turns it into honey. Even when our present is bitter—and in this age it often is—our future is sweet.[7]

Honey represents God's law and God's word. David says that the rules of the Lord which warn and guide us are "sweeter also than honey and drippings of the honeycomb" (Ps. 19:10). The psalmist sings to God, "How sweet are your words to my taste, sweeter than honey to my mouth!" (Ps. 119:103). Both Ezekiel and John describe visions in which they eat the scroll of God's word and it tastes as sweet as honey in their mouths (Ezek. 3:3; Rev. 10:9–10). So reading and reflecting on Scripture is like plunging your spoon, your dipper, or perhaps even your hand into the syrupy depths of a honeycomb to scoop out and eat the contents. The Word of God is rich, tasty, satisfying, and enjoyable. It brightens the eyes and enlivens the soul. It does not need any flavorings or preservatives to make it taste better, and you cannot add to it or take away from it. It lasts through the centuries and never goes out of date. You and I can take the portions of Scripture that archaeologists have found in caves, even thousands of years ago, and they are just as enlivening today as they were when they were first written. In a world filled with processed products and hybrid wisdom, the words of God are pure, golden, and luxuriously sweet without even trying.

Honey represents God's gifts and God's grace. The first time we encounter honey in the Bible, it is as a gift, given by one person to gain favor with another. This pattern recurs several times: from Jacob to Joseph (Gen. 43:11), from the people of Mahanaim to David (2 Sam. 17:27–29), from Jeroboam to Ahijah (1 Kings 14:3), and from Israel to God (2 Chron. 31:5). But when God gives honey to us, it is not to find favor with us or to trade it for something else. God doesn't need anything from anybody. Rather he gives honey—and his gracious gifts in general—simply to bless. It is hard to think of two more unmerited, one-sided gifts in the Bible than manna, which God (literally) produces out of the clear blue sky, and the water that gushes forth from the rock in the wilderness. In neither case does Israel do anything; they simply arrive somewhere, moaning and exhausted, and God provides immeasurably more than they can ask or imagine. So it may be significant that the manna tastes of honey (Ex. 16:31) and the water is later described as "honey from the rock" (Ps. 81:16). Honey, it seems, is a symbol of the abundant sweetness of God's gracious gifts, which cannot be earned, horse-traded, bought, or exchanged. It can only be received.

We are called not just to learn about God but to experience him. We are invited to taste his sweetness and allow his golden richness—beautifully expressed in his rescue, his Word, and his grace—to brighten our eyes and refresh our souls. "Oh, taste and see that the LORD is good!" (Ps. 34:8).

CHAPTER

10

SEX

THE LOVE OF GOD

I came to my garden, my sister, my bride,
I gathered my myrrh with my spice,
I ate my honeycomb with my honey,
I drank my wine with my milk.

Eat, friends, drink,
and be drunk with love!

—SONG OF SOLOMON 5:1

first read the Song of Solomon when I was about ten, and
descended into fits of giggles. I was in a religious studies class at
school, and we all had Bibles on our desks, and one of my friends
discovered the most sensual, illicit, smirk-inducing section in

the entire book. (Looking back on it now, this cannot have been a coincidence; he must have had it shown to him by a mischievous parent.) We struck gold that day. We would peer down at his copy, try in vain to suppress laughter at verses such as "Your stature is like a palm tree, and your breasts are like its clusters. I say I will climb the palm tree and lay hold of its fruit" (Song 7:7–8), and then rummage through our own Bibles to see if they contained the same passage. When we found it, we would fall about laughing again and show it to our neighbor on the other side to spread the joy, and so it continued. Mr. Cripps didn't even get cross about it. I expect he'd seen it all before.

I don't react to the Song that way anymore. I have heard sermons and read books on it, studied it in my devotional times, and come to see how mysterious, rich, and beautiful it is. I have seen how it celebrates both sexual love in marriage and the romance between God and his people that sexual love in marriage is designed to reflect.

But I often think back to my ten-year-old reaction, because in a silly, boyish way, it reflects two things about sex and God that are just as true for adults as they are for children. One: it is genuinely remarkable that God loves the romance, poetry, mystery, and physicality of sex so much that he included a song about it in the Bible. God's view of sex is clearly higher than we think, whether that discovery prompts embarrassment, amusement, or worshipful gratitude. Two: by contrast, our view of sex is clearly lower than we think. Although we live in a society that prides itself on having a positive view of sex, our cultural representations of it are far more likely to generate cheap simulation or childish snickers than the unashamed, bold, beautiful celebration of sexual intimacy that you find in the Song. As sex gets commoditized, it becomes shallow, diluted, trivialized, which leads in the end to people finding it less meaningful rather than more. I often think of the student who was asked by feminist Naomi Wolf whether rushing into bed with people removed the mystery of sex. "Mystery?" the student replied. "I don't know what you're talking about. Sex has no mystery."[8]

This diminishment of sex to the point of triviality comes, in part, through asking the wrong questions. In the contemporary West, as reflected in both mainstream popular culture and pornography, the predominant sexual questions are how (technique, frequency, position, enhancements) and where (location, environment). Religious and moralistic responses often address this by focusing on who (the right person, "the one," your life partner) and when (after commitment and/or marriage). Each of these questions has its place, and each is addressed to some degree in the Song. But the crucial questions, from a Christian point of view, are what sex is and why God created it.

God is spirit and does not have sexual organs. Even when he takes on flesh, and sexual organs, in the person of Jesus, he remains single and celibate. He could perfectly well have created humans to reproduce asexually (like most bacteria) or without making contact with each other (like most plants) or in functional ways that aim simply at reproduction rather than pleasure (like most animals). Yet instead he gave us the gift of having sex in the most intimate and emotionally rich way possible. He created our sexual organs to fit, the male inside the female. He gave women a body part whose only purpose is to enhance her sexual enjoyment. And he inspired a book of the Bible to celebrate the whole extravaganza. This book is a rich and explicit poem that takes delight in touching and kissing, lips and hair, curves and strength. Why? What is sex—what does it mean, represent, embody for us—that God should have made it like this?

An obvious answer, and one we should not overlook, is that the primary purpose of sex is to have children, and everything that makes it delightful—physical, emotional, hormonal, spiritual—is designed to strengthen the bond between husband and wife and enable us to face the challenges of pregnancy, birth, and parenthood together. It is easy to forget this in a society in which it is so common to have sex without children (through contraception) and children without sex (through IVF), but it is clearly foundational to what sex is for, from "be fruitful and multiply" (Gen. 1:28) onward. Sex points toward children, biblically speaking. To make love is to give yourself up, not just to the person before you but to the little person who may come after you.

That, if you like, is the relational answer to the questions of what sex is and why God made it this way. But Scripture provides us with theological answers as well. Three in particular stand out.

Sex is about creation. Think for a moment about Genesis 1: the entire structure of creation is made up of complementary pairs, which are distinguished from one another as part of God's creative design. In the beginning, the earth is "formless and empty" (v. 2 NIV), and God's creative work consists of making distinctions between things, or separating things, to bring about order and life. We get light and dark, day and night, heaven and earth, land and sea, sun and moon, male and female. Sex—which until very recently just meant "male" or "female" rather than "sexual intercourse"—mirrors the one-to-one harmony, the complementarity, the "fit," that exists throughout creation.

We don't have one sun and many moons, or two days for every night; we have one of each. We don't get life if we have earth above and earth below (which is basically what a cave is) or sky above and sky below (which is basically what a gas giant like Jupiter is); we get life through having one of each, with the sky above producing water and the earth below receiving it and bearing forth life. (I'm guessing the sexual parallels don't need a diagram.) And just as male and female are separated in creation, with a view to being united again in marriage, so the heavens and the earth, though separated for now, will ultimately be united in cosmic marriage in the new creation. Two will become one, and those whom God has joined together, let no one separate.

Sex is also about worship. Biblically, there is a connection between the number of gods you worship and the number of sexual partners you have. The Ten Commandments demand an exclusive approach to worship ("You shall have no other gods but me") and an exclusive approach to sexuality (effectively, "You shall have no other husbands/wives but him/her"). When Israel violates one, from the golden calf incident onward, she usually violates the other. The book of Hosea develops this image in particularly graphic detail, picturing God as a faithful husband and Israel as his promiscuous wife, but many other biblical writers present idolatry as an act of sexual immorality with other gods. "They whored after other gods and bowed down to them" (Judg. 2:17). Paul makes the point that idolatry is mirrored in sexual immorality, with both involving the abandonment of one God/partner who is different from you, in exchange for many gods/partners who are the same as you. Our sexuality reflects our worship. Faithfulness in one reflects faithfulness in the other.

And sex is about the gospel. Sexual relations, shared between a husband and a wife within the context of marriage, offer a profound parable of the Christian message. "'A man shall leave his father and mother and hold fast to his wife,'" says Paul, "'and the two shall become one flesh.' This mystery is profound, and I am saying that it refers to Christ and the church" (Eph. 5:31–32). We make promises, we forsake all others, we exchange rings, we celebrate with a meal, we share all our worldly possessions, we take on a new family name, and then we have sex as a physical seal of our commitment, trusting that out of it God will bring forth new life and celebrating our union with and surrender to one another and to God.

Each of those steps preaches the gospel. Jesus promises never to leave us or abandon us. We promise to forsake all other gods as long as we live. He gives us a gift that seals the covenant (his Holy Spirit), and he provides a meal for us to celebrate with the whole family (bread and wine). All his possessions become ours, and all our debts become his. We take on his name. We enter into union with Christ and get baptized in water as a physical seal of our commitment, trusting that out of it God will bring forth new life and celebrating our union with and surrender to one another.

Which takes us full circle, back to the Song of Solomon. Sex is a beautiful thing, a loving gift from a bountiful and abundant God. But it is not an ultimate thing. It is a shadow, a parable, a silhouette, whose true fulfillment is found in the love that God has for his people, and it is this that makes it mysterious, meaningful, and transcendent.

Many find it surprising when they discover how much of our richest teaching on sexuality, marriage, and new creation comes from single people. John the friend of the bridegroom (John 3:29), Paul the best man (2 Cor. 11:2), Jesus himself, and countless priests, popes, monks, nuns, and other single believers have spent decades reflecting on, praying for, and anticipating the wedding of Christ and the church.

In many ways, however, it is not surprising at all. Married people, assuming that sex is fundamentally there for us and our spouse, can get so preoccupied with the picture that we forget the ultimate reality, like someone at Victoria Falls watching video footage of it on their phone. Single people often know better. Sex is a signpost. It is but a glimpse of a relationship, a union, and a happiness that are grander and deeper than our wildest imagining. "Eat, friends, drink, and be drunk with love!" (Song 5:1).

CHAPTER

11

MOUNTAINS

THE COVENANTS OF GOD

It shall come to pass in the latter days
*that the mountain of the house of the L*ORD
shall be established as the highest of the
mountains,
and shall be lifted up above the hills;
and all the nations shall flow to it,
and many peoples shall come, and say:
*"Come, let us go up to the mountain of the L*ORD*,*
to the house of the God of Jacob."
—ISAIAH 2:2-3

Kangchenjunga is the third-highest mountain in the world, but you've probably never heard of it. Most of us have heard of Everest and K2, and maybe several other peaks worldwide: Kilimanjaro, Aconcagua, Denali, Mont Blanc, the Matterhorn, and others. But by and large, Kangchenjunga flies under the radar.

This is remarkable for several reasons. It is breathtakingly beautiful. Its remoteness means that trekkers and climbers have generally avoided it, which has preserved its pristine and untainted appearance. Rising to a height of 8,586 meters (28,169 feet), it was believed to be the highest mountain in the world until the 1850s. It is composed of five peaks in two countries, hence its name (in Tibetan, Kangchenjunga means "the five treasures of the great snow"). Most intriguing, its summit has never been reached, not because it is physically impossible to attain but because the first climbers promised the Chogyal, the local monarch, that it would remain undisturbed, and all subsequent groups have followed the tradition. Kangchenjunga is a giant and beautiful mountain with five distinct peaks, spanning national borders and towering over its neighbors, a mountain that most people have never thought about, the summit of which has never been fully scaled. We'll come back to that in a minute.

If you read the Scriptures with mountains in mind, you will quickly notice how often they appear. The word mountain appears in the Bible more often than the words cross, grace, and gospel put together. If you've ever traveled in Israel, you may find this surprising. The territory is not exactly alpine; there is a mountain range of sorts running north to south down the middle, but its highest point would be one of the lowest points in Colorado, and much of the country is made up of coastal plains (to the west), the Negev Desert (to the south), and the

Jordan Valley (to the east). Even Mount Carmel, the site of Elijah's famous showdown with the prophets of Baal, is only the height of One World Trade Center.

Mountains, however, are mentioned so often not because of their geographical prominence but because of their theological significance. They matter because of what they represent: giant obstacles that only God can move (Zech. 4:7) or longevity (Prov. 8:25) or apparent stability (Ps. 46:2) or challenges that require great faith (Mark 11:23). Most important, they are places where people encounter God. When God appears to his people, he frequently does so on a mountain, thus communicating a combination of height and exaltation, grandeur and beauty, proximity to the heavens and supremacy over the earth.

Mountains communicate the distance between us and God. Ascending them requires that we make preparation well in advance, to make sure we are not incapacitated or even killed by the conditions or change in pressure (as I discovered to my own cost when I ascended the Sierra Nevada too quickly in a car and very nearly collapsed in a light-headed, oxygen-starved heap). By summoning people to meet him at the summit, God reminds us how other than us he is, how much needs to be done in order for us to encounter him, and how dangerous it is to approach him flippantly. "Who shall ascend the hill of the LORD?" (Ps. 24:3).

Yet mountains are also places of grace. Mountaintop encounters with God are moments not just of distance or challenge but of presence, commission, and sacrifice. We ascend toward him, but at the same time he descends toward us. Mountains are places of revelation, of promise, of covenant. All five of the major covenants in the Old Testament—via Adam, Noah, Abraham, Moses, and David—are associated with mountains.

God's covenant purposes are like Kangchenjunga: five distinct treasures all forming one giant, beautiful whole. Most people may have never thought about them, but they span national borders and tower over their neighbors, and their summit has never been fully scaled.

The first covenant mountain is in Eden. (The word mountain is not used in Genesis 1–3, but Ezekiel 28:13–14 calls it "the holy mountain of God.") Human beings, looking down over the abundant foothills and knowing that God has given them every place the light touches, are commissioned to fill the earth and subdue it and promised life if they obey and death if they don't. This is base camp, if you like. The covenant with Adam does not reach the same heights as the peaks which follow—it is often referred to as the "covenant of works," as opposed to the later "covenant of grace"—but it is the one we discover first, and visiting it is essential if we are to reach any of the others.

The second is Mount Ararat. Noah steps out of the ark onto a mountainside, his family having been saved from judgment simply because he found favor in the eyes of the Lord (Gen. 6:8), and God immediately makes a second covenant. Like Adam, Noah is commissioned to be fruitful and multiply and given examples of things he can eat (animals) and not eat (blood). But with these conditions comes a promise: "Never again shall all flesh be cut off by the waters of the flood" (9:11). And with that promise comes a sign: "I have set my bow in the cloud" (v. 13). God commits himself to deal with sin without the most obvious and drastic solution—destroying everyone—and he hangs up his military bow in the sky as a permanent reminder. How exactly he *will* deal with sin, and rescue his creation from evil and death, is not yet revealed.

It becomes clearer at Mount Moriah. Abraham has already received astonishing promises from God (a land, an everlasting inheritance, a child, an innumerably large family) when he is told to sacrifice his only son, and with him all hope of God's promises coming to pass. In an act of heartrending obedience, he binds Isaac to the altar, only to find that God has already prepared a substitute for him and that because of his obedience, God is guaranteeing with an oath that Abraham will be blessed, fruitful, triumphant, and a means of blessing to the entire world. This mountain's strange fusion—of substitutionary sacrifice, a father willing to give up his only son, and an offspring in whom the whole world will find blessing—must have prompted Abraham to wonder. Considered from generations later, as one of five covenant mountains of increasing majesty, Mount Moriah makes his innumerable offspring marvel.

So does the next one, Mount Sinai. We often think of Sinai merely as a mountain of law, thunder, judgment, and fire, remembering the covenant's obligations rather than its promises. There are of course obligations, as there are with any covenant. But the promises are glorious: "You shall be my treasured possession among all peoples, for all the earth is mine; and you shall be to me a kingdom of priests and a holy nation" (Ex. 19:5–6). If Mount Ararat made us wonder how God would rescue the world without destroying everyone, and Mount Moriah showed us that it would be through the offspring of Abraham, Mount Sinai shows that it will come through the nation of Israel, serving the world as kings and priests. When the people of Israel finally enter the promised land, they are to declare the blessings and curses of this covenant from (you've guessed it) two mountains (Deut. 27:11–13).

The fifth covenant mountain is Mount Zion, the site of Jerusalem and the location of the temple, where the expansive promises to Abraham's offspring and the nation of Israel are focused like a laser onto one individual. The solution to the world's problems will not ultimately come through everyone descended from Abraham, or everyone in the nation of Israel, or even everyone in the tribe of Judah; it will come from one specific descendant of King David, to whom will be given a house, a name, a throne, the steadfast love of God, and an everlasting kingdom (2 Sam. 7:12–16). We are not given his name. We get a few more clues in the rest of the Old Testament: birth in Bethlehem (Mic. 5:2), a virgin mother (Isa. 7:14), ministry in Galilee (Isa. 9:1), foreshadowing by an Elijah figure (Mal. 4:5). But as the prophets fall silent, we are still waiting, not just for a new king but for a new covenant (Jer. 31:31–34).

It is only when Jesus finally arrives that we are able to see how Kangchenjunga's five peaks are all part of one giant mountain. Christ fulfills five covenants at once: Eden's by defying the devil's garden temptations, Ararat's by committing to love his enemies rather than destroy them all, Moriah's by offering himself as a willing substitute, Sinai's by serving the world as the perfect priest-king, and Zion's by establishing an everlasting kingdom. As the Gospels (especially Matthew) point out, he is continually going up and down mountains. He teaches on one, prays on one, is transfigured on one, gets betrayed on one, is crucified on one, and ascends into heaven from one. Some passages even suggest that he will return on one.[9]

Fittingly, the final scene of the final book of the Bible is viewed from "a great, high mountain" (Rev. 21:10). Revelation is filled with images from all five covenants and all five mountains, merrily dancing between pictures of gardens, rivers, and life-giving trees (like Eden), seas and rainbows (like Ararat), substitutionary sheep (like Moriah), thunder and fire and clouds and trumpets (like Sinai), and thrones and temples (like Zion). But they have all been made one, and they have all been made new. On that day we will all say with the prophet, "Come, let us go up to the mountain of the LORD, to the house of the God of Jacob" (Isa. 2:3).

CHAPTER

12

GARDENS

~~~~~~

THE PRESENCE OF GOD

*"They shall come and sing aloud on the height of Zion,
    and they shall be radiant over the goodness of
        the LORD,
over the grain, the wine, and the oil,
    and over the young of the flock and the herd;
their life shall be like a watered garden,
    and they shall languish no more."*

—JEREMIAH 31:12

One of the most self-defeating openings in modern literature comes at the beginning of Richard Dawkins's *The God Delusion*. Released in 2006, this fiery atheist manifesto was wildly popular, selling more than three million copies and receiving breathless endorsements from a variety of cultural icons. It made a trenchant case for the idea that belief in God is groundless, pitiful, anti-intellectual, and dangerous and suggested that theists—and Christians in particular—are driven to such absurdity by wickedness, idiocy, mental illness, or a combination of all three.

In some ways the book was actually quite good. It was written with clarity, punch, wit, and humor; it was timely, coming as it did five years after 9/11 and three years after Western troops had invaded Iraq, prompting escalating religious rhetoric on both sides; and much of it was clearly true.[10] Unfortunately, the bits that were clearly not true were so bad that they scuppered the whole thing, as many critics pointed out at the time.[11] And the book has the unusual distinction of refuting itself before it even begins. The epigraph, which appears before the contents page, is a quotation from the author Douglas Adams: "Isn't it enough to see that a garden is beautiful without having to believe that there are fairies at the bottom of it too?"

It's a fascinating question. Our first instinct is to agree: the existence of a beautiful garden does not in any way require a belief in fairies. Depending on who we are, this might prompt smug reassurance, thoughtful beard-stroking, or blind panic. But after a moment's thought, this reaction is followed by a second response. No, gardens do not make us believe in fairies. But they do make us believe in another class of beings, who offer a far closer analogy to belief in God than fairies ever could. They make us believe in beings whose design, creative activity, and ongoing care are responsible for the land resembling a beautiful garden rather than a wasteland or a jungle or an overgrown, weed-infested mess. *Gardeners.*

Without knowing it, Douglas Adams and Richard Dawkins have taken our belief in a powerful, intelligent, caring designer whom we cannot currently see and tried to debunk it by referring to something—a beautiful garden—that requires belief in a powerful, intelligent, caring designer whom we cannot currently see. In doing so, they have not just sawn off the argumentative branch they are sitting on, by acknowledging that the world points beyond itself to a creator; they have also (unwittingly) drawn attention to an important biblical theme: God is a gardener.

We know this from the second chapter of Scripture. "The LORD God planted a garden in Eden, in the east" (Gen. 2:8), and this garden is complete with trees, fruits, vegetables, flowers, rivers, minerals, onyx, gold, birds, animals, human beings, marriage, sex, life, and the presence of God himself (vv. 9–25). It is not just lush and idyllic—the Greek word for garden here, *paradeisos*, gives us our word paradise—but enormous as well, and probably mountainous, given that it serves as the source for four rivers. It is more like a primeval Yosemite than a vegetable patch or a manicured lawn. By planting a garden, placing humanity in it, and walking alongside them in the cool of the day, God is showing us the connection between his creativity, his love, his abundance (every tree that was pleasant to the eye and good for food, every beast of the field, every living creature, and so on), and above all his presence. Eden is a place of life, love, and harmony because God lives there. The first garden is a temple, and from now on all temples will be gardens.

That might sound like a stretch, until we study the designs of the tabernacle and the temple in detail (which, since they are lengthy and a bit repetitive, most of us don't). They are full of garden imagery, pointing us to the verdant, lush, life-giving bounty of the gardener God who lives there. Consider: the temple is made out of cedar trees, "carved in the form of gourds and open flowers," and the floor is boarded with cypress (1 Kings 6:15–18). Like Eden, it is guarded by cherubim, built on a mountain, entered from the east, and adorned with gold and onyx (1 Chron. 29:2). The doors of the sanctuary are made of olivewood, carved with palm trees and flowers in bloom (1 Kings 6:31–32). The bronze pillars are festooned with hundreds of pomegranates, and "on the tops of the pillars was lily-work" (7:20–22). The panels are set with livestock (oxen) and wild beasts (lions), and as you walk across the court, you find yourself surrounded by fresh water (vv. 23–29). There is a tree-shaped lampstand outside the Holy of Holies, and a further ten made of pure gold (v. 49). It would have felt like an orchard, a well-watered garden, a *paradeisos*. It spoke to Israel: the God of the garden lives here. Welcome.

So gardens are places of abundance and divine presence. But they are also places of romance and love. The first marriage and the first love song took place in a garden (Gen. 2:18–25), and this profound mystery is a picture of the love between Christ and the church (Eph. 5:31–32). Numerous biblical couples get together in garden-like places, under trees or at wells or both. The Song of Solomon is full of plants, trees, flowers, orchards, fruits, fountains, and gardens, reinforcing the connection between our intimacy with God and our intimacy with one another. This connection, interestingly, is still reflected today, every time a couple gets married surrounded by carnations, arbors, garlands, lilies, trellises, and petals of confetti. We design our wedding venues like a garden of love, not least because we first knew love in a garden.

Yet the garden is also a place of tragedy. We do not just

remember paradise; we remember paradise lost. Eden was not just the garden of love but the garden of love spurned. Life was rejected in favor of the knowledge of good and evil, marriage was spoiled, and verdant abundance became thorns and thistles and pain in childbirth. As human beings, we were meant to take the garden with us, filling the earth with the life and harmony we found there, but instead we were exiled from it, frog-marched out by the eastern exit, with cherubim on guard to prevent us from coming back. From that day on, we lost our unrestricted access to the presence of God, both in the temple-like garden and in the garden-like temple. We have been pining for it ever since. The human story has been a long and often disastrous series of attempts to get back to the garden.

It is fitting, then—as well as glorious beyond words—that our access back into the garden, with all the abundance and presence and love that goes with it, was secured in two gardens. The first, which we know as the garden of Gethsemane, reversed the decision of Eden, replacing Adam's "not your will but mine" with Christ's "not my will but yours." The second, as Jesus stepped out of the tomb just a couple of days later, reversed the consequences of Eden. Where Adam brought death to everyone in a garden and then went to hide, Christ brought life to everyone in a garden and then made himself as visible as possible. This connection may be what John is hinting at when he says that Mary thought Jesus was the gardener (John 20:15). In more ways than one, he was.

The result, as Jesus had said while being crucified, is that those who trust him can be brought back to God. "Today you will be with me in [*paradeisos*]" (Luke 23:43). We are welcomed into the abundance and vitality of a new and better Eden. The cherubim blocking your way have been stood down. The serpent has been crushed. The garden of love is open, and the Gardener has been preparing a place for you. When we finally see it, in the final two chapters of Scripture, we get the most delightful sense of déjà vu—there is a river and a tree and leaves and fruit and gold and onyx and a wedding. And in the midst of it all is God himself, so bright that there is no need for the sun, and so present that there is no need for a temple (Rev. 21:22–23). Welcome home.

CHAPTER
13

RAINBOWS

THE FAITHFULNESS OF GOD

> *Like the appearance of the bow that is in the cloud*
> *on the day of rain, so was the appearance of the*
> *brightness all around.*
>
> *Such was the appearance of the likeness of the*
> *glory of the LORD. And when I saw it, I fell on my*
> *face, and I heard the voice of one speaking.*
>
> **—EZEKIEL 1:28**

There is more to a rainbow than meets the eye.

In one sense I mean that literally. The human eye cannot see the colors at either end of the spectrum, despite the pictures you see in children's Bibles, and there are around a million shades and hues that are too subtle for us to distinguish from each other. But in another sense I mean it symbolically. The rainbow carries a number of meanings in Christian thought, and many of us are blind to several of them (a blindness which is probably made worse because the symbol has recently come to mean something quite different, so we may not think about it so much). Biblically, there are at least five meanings to the rainbow, and each one reveals something important about God and his people.

First, rainbows mean beauty. This is the one that strikes everybody who has ever seen one, whether or not they have ever heard of Noah. Few things in creation can compare to the beauty of sunbeams colliding with waterfall spray, as refracted shards of color scatter in all directions. When Ezekiel is trying to describe the indescribable—"the appearance of the likeness of the glory of the LORD"—he draws on the most splendid images in creation, from an expanse of glittering crystal to an emerald throne, but culminates in the dazzling brightness of "the bow that is in the cloud on the day of rain" (Ezek. 1:28). The glory of God, insofar as we can see it, looks like a man of fire on a jeweled throne surrounded by rainbows. Simply by being there, rainbows testify to the abundant beauty of the God who makes them.

Their gorgeous appearance results from the fact that they show us unity in diversity. In a rainbow, one color (white) is shown to be many (red, indigo, yellow, green, and the rest), and many come together into one. That fusion of color is one way of looking at the doctrine of the church in Revelation. The people of God are pictured as warriors, witnesses, worshipers, and wedding guests, all dressed in white, and yet at the same time, they appear as a multicolored, multiethnic multitude, a city adorned by precious stones of all colors, from jasper to sapphire, emerald to amethyst. (This point is obscured today because we use the word white to refer to people who patently aren't. Nobody called themselves white until the seventeenth century, and when they did, it was partly to lay claim to the idea of purity. But if you put my skin on a color palette, it would be classified as peach in the winter and beige in the summer.) Viewed from one perspective, the people of God are one color; viewed from another, they represent every color on the spectrum. The church is the true rainbow nation, the place where people are many and one at the same time.

Staying in Revelation for a moment, rainbows also reflect unapproachable light. In biblical appearances of God, we often find two images: the sun and clouds. The sun speaks of the dazzling radiance of God, the brilliant light of his purity, excellence, and perfection. Clouds speak of the hiddenness, the concealed majesty, of the immortal, invisible, only wise God whom no one has seen or can see. But when light and unapproachability come together—when the midday sun shines brightly through thick cloud cover—you get an explosion of rainbows. That is why, when John first sees the Holy One enthroned in heaven, "around the throne was a rainbow that had the appearance of an emerald" (Rev. 4:3). That is what unapproachable light looks like.

For all this, the only explicit meaning given to the rainbow in Scripture is as a sign of God's covenant. "God said, 'This is the sign of the covenant that I make between me and you and every living creature that is with you, for all future generations: I have set my bow in the cloud, and it shall be a sign of the covenant between me and the earth'" (Gen. 9:12–13). Covenants in Scripture are accompanied by signs: circumcision, Sabbath, bread and wine, and in this case a rainbow. It signifies a covenant made not just with God's people but with creation itself: a commitment never again to destroy all flesh in a flood. But unlike most other biblical covenants, in which we have to do something, this one is entirely one-sided. The rainbow appears in the sky unilaterally, gratuitously, and with no response on our part required or even possible. You may be obeying God faithfully or disobeying him flagrantly, but next time the sun breaks through on a rainy day, there will be a rainbow, and nothing you do (or fail to do) will be able to hold it back. Rainbows are reminders of a foundational reality. No matter what we do, God is faithful. He always keeps his promises.

Finally, rainbows mean peace. Consider that phrase again: "I have set my bow in the cloud." Biblical Hebrew doesn't have a word for rainbow, so the word used here is simply bow, the regular word for a weapon that fires arrows. So this is God's announcement that he is hanging up his bow, holstering his weapon, and committing not just to limiting the rainfall but to bringing peace to all of creation. It immediately raises the question, how? How will God destroy evil and live at peace with humanity at the same time? And that question forms the backdrop to every subsequent covenant, until the day when the God of the rainbow takes flesh, breaks bread, and passes round a cup containing the blood of the new covenant, poured out for many for the forgiveness of sins.

We may be able to go one step farther. If the rainbow was in fact a bow, then the archer would have to pull the string downward, toward the earth, and then the arrow would be fired upward, away from the world and "up into the heart of heaven."[12] The God of the rainbow brought peace not by ignoring all of our violence and strife but by letting it all be aimed at him and allowing himself to be pierced through the heart by the hatred and aggression of human beings. Then, having emptied the quiver once and for all, he lowered his bow to extend his arms out in welcome.

Rainbows speak of perfection, plurality, purity, promises, and peace. Next time you see one, pause. Reflect. And consider the beauty, faithfulness, and multicolored wisdom of the God who made it.

CHAPTER

14

DONKEYS

THE PEACE OF GOD

Rejoice greatly, O daughter of Zion!
Shout aloud, O daughter of Jerusalem!
Behold, your king is coming to you;
righteous and having salvation is he,
humble and mounted on a donkey,
on a colt, the foal of a donkey.

—ZECHARIAH 9:9

I've been asked about the problem of evil many times, but my answer has never involved donkeys. Or ostriches. Or the birthing habits of mountain goats or the possibility of plowing with wild oxen. Pointing out the wildness, stubbornness, and sheer ridiculousness of certain animals would not seem to me the obvious way to go in defending God's justice. It would seem trivial or flippant, when faced with a suffering and grieving individual, to start talking about how ostriches forget where their eggs are and accidentally tread on them or how donkeys wander off and cannot be brought back for love nor money.

Yet that's what God does in Job 39. Having listened for thirty-seven chapters to five people debating his justice and the problem of suffering, God finally speaks. This is the moment Job, and we as readers, and everyone who has ever wondered about the goodness of God, have all been waiting for, and he says something utterly unexpected. The first bit of his response, about the sky and the weather (Job 38), is surprising but effective; it is both reassuring and challenging to be reminded of God's sovereignty over the sea, the snow, and the stars. But then he spends three chapters talking about animals. Not just any animals: *weird* animals. Behemoth (chap. 40) and Leviathan (chap. 41), animals so strange that we still don't know what they are. Some people get very excited about whether they might be dinosaurs (they aren't), and miss the point entirely. And in chapter 39, a bizarre parade of pregnant goats, runaway donkeys, wild oxen, ignorant ostriches, warhorses, hawks, and eagles. Even my study Bible is baffled by it. Job 39 gets less explanation than any other chapter in Scripture.

God's point in this quirky zoology lesson is to show Job how limited his knowledge is. You have no idea when a pregnant goat is about to give birth (39:1–3). You have no control over the wild donkey, who "scorns the tumult of the city" and "hears not the shouts of the driver" (v. 7). You don't have the power to make ostriches foolish, cruel, clumsy, and yet fast enough to outrun a horse (vv. 13–18). But I do. Perhaps your perspective on the world is more limited than you realize.[13]

Behind this, though, is another observation it would be easy to miss. God deliberately created some animals to be funny, clumsy, untamable, exasperating, oafish, whimsical, and just plain silly. He did it on purpose. The eccentricity of an ostrich, in all its egg-crushing, head-burying, flightless glory, is divinely designed. Every time a donkey makes a trainer throw their hands up in frustration, God chuckles with delight.

Given how few animals Job would have known about, in a world without global travel or nature programs, it is safe to assume that Job 39 is just the start of it. Behold the duck-billed platypus, which I made as I made you. Consider the implausible squareness of the Tibetan fox's face. The contemptuous arrogance of the cat. The tottering shuffle of the emperor penguin, which calls out for Laurel and Hardy background music. The way porcupines have sex. The fussy orderliness of a beaver. The geometry of the flamingo, which not only stands on one leg despite having two of them but is so out of proportion that it looks like a swan that has had a bamboo rod inserted into it and been dyed pink. The way a sloth takes an hour to get to the toilet and back. The prancing, exhibitionist skirt-raising of a male bird of paradise, and the crestfallen expression he makes when his advances are rejected. What does it say about God's ceaseless creativity that he made so many animals like this, just for fun? What does it say about his sense of humor?

Still, it is hard to beat the donkey. (When I googled "funniest animals" just now, the first one to appear was a donkey. Despite all the options available, I wasn't remotely surprised, and I suspect you aren't either.) The teeth, the ears, the hee-haw, the sense we get that it is basically a poor man's horse, and the sense that it knows we all think that and decides to get its own back by being selectively uncooperative. When King Midas offended Apollo, he was given the ears of an ass. When God wanted to expose the foolishness of trying to prophesy against his people, he arranged for a donkey to rebuke the false prophet in question (Num. 22:28–30). Even the word itself is faintly ridiculous, and in many languages the equivalent of *ass* is used to insult people for stupidity or incompetence. It does not take much imagination to see why.

Yet this is the animal on which Jesus Christ, God incarnate, rode into Jerusalem to save the world. Not a horse, an ass. Not a charger at war, a beast of burden. Not in pomp and ceremony, in humility and service. It's as if the president of the United States were to leave the limousines and Suburbans in the garage on Inauguration Day and drive down the National Mall in a milk float.[14]

Ironically, we refer to this moment as the triumphal entry, drawing our phrase from the Roman *triumphus*, the victory parade in which conquering commanders would ride into cities after killing their enemies. But this is precisely what Jesus was not doing. If he had wanted to do that, he would have ridden into town on a white horse, with a robe dipped in blood—which is just how Revelation 19 describes his return in the future—and everyone would have understood. Instead he rode on a donkey, an animal as temperamentally unsuitable for warfare as you can imagine. He was very specific about it, telling two of his disciples, "Go into the village in front of you, and immediately you will find a donkey tied, and a colt with her. Untie them and bring them to me" (Matt. 21:2).

This was not novel. Donkeys were royal animals in ancient Israel, and rulers had frequently ridden them before. The sons of Jair, and later those of Abdon, all rode donkeys (Judg. 10:4; 12:14). The sons of King David all rode mules (2 Sam. 13:29). Solomon was proclaimed king as he rode on a mule (1 Kings 1:33); the symbolism was so familiar that his scheming brother Adonijah, who was in the middle of a botched attempt at a coup, immediately knew the game was up (1 Kings 1:41–44). Zechariah had promised that Israel's king would return to her riding on a donkey (Zech. 9:9). Sometimes, in our eagerness to show the difference between Jesus and all other kings, we imply he is so different that people wouldn't have realized he was a king at all. Far from it. Kings rode donkeys, and everyone who had read their Scriptures would know that.

So the crowds who saw Jesus ride into Jerusalem on that afternoon in April would have recognized what was going on. This was the Messiah, Israel's king, or at least someone claiming to be, hence all the palm branches and cloaks and quotations from Psalm 118. But he was riding on a donkey, because he was coming in peace. This, Zechariah had immediately explained, is why the Messiah's choice of animal would be significant: "I will cut off the chariot from Ephraim and the war horse from Jerusalem; and the battle bow shall be cut off, and he shall speak peace to the nations" (Zech. 9:10). He was coming in humility and service, "humble and mounted on a donkey" (v. 9). He was armed with words of peace, not weapons of war. This king, slowly wobbling into Jerusalem as the crowds cried Hosanna, was not coming to wash in the blood of his enemies. He was coming to wash the feet of his friends.

I said at the start of this chapter that most of us, myself

included, would never think of answering the problem of evil with a donkey. But by entering Jerusalem on one and thereby promising to save his people not through violence and war but in humility and peace, that is exactly what Jesus did. *Shalom.*

CHAPTER

15

SUN

THE PRIMACY OF GOD

"For you who fear my name, the sun of
righteousness shall rise with healing in its wings.
You shall go out leaping like calves from the stall."

—MALACHI 4:2

I have never been able to understand why anyone would worship a wooden statue. Or a tree or an Asherah pole, a cow or an elephant, or a god who looks like a frog. I think I get it at an intellectual level—they represent fertility or whatever—but I cannot get my head around people being spiritually drawn to adore them, rejoice before them, or sacrifice to them. If I had been born an ancient pagan, I wouldn't have been the idol-fashioning, maypole-dancing type. (At least, I struggle to imagine myself that way.)

But I can see why people used to worship the sun. I'm not saying they should have, obviously, but I can relate to the instinct. So far as anyone knew until quite recently, the sun was by far the largest thing in the sky, and the source of all light, heat, power, and life. Especially in Northern Europe, where I come from, the difference between sunshine and darkness, summer and winter, is so great that it must have been tempting to rush outside in the springtime and prostrate yourself before the giant yellow ball of fire. Were it not for Christianity, I suspect many of us still would.

Unsurprisingly, this presented a challenge to ancient Israel. Moses had to urge the people not to worship the sun, with fairly drastic legal consequences for anyone who did (Deut. 4:19; 17:2–5), and the prophets reveal that it was still a problem many centuries later (Jer. 8:2; Ezek. 8:16). The risk of idolatry is partly why Scripture keeps pointing out all the things the sun is not. It is not eternal: the Bible's opening chapter makes clear that the sun was not created until day four, and its last chapter tells us that the sun is no longer needed, "for the Lord God will be their light" (Rev. 22:5). It is not inevitable and can be darkened (and dethroned) at will by the One who created it (Ex. 10:21–29). It is not in control; it can be made to stand still (Josh. 10:12–14) or to move shadows in the wrong direction (Isa. 38:8). These might look like random potshots at the sun, but they are ways of protecting Israel from turning a gift into an idol. The sun had the potential to be a huge theological problem.

Yet it also had the potential to be a huge theological opportunity. So long as people could use the sun as a way of meditating on and worshiping God, rather than as something to be meditated on and worshiped itself, they could learn a great deal about him. The psalmist is very happy to use the sun to shed light on the nature of God: "The LORD God is a sun and shield" (Ps. 84:11).

There are numerous attributes of God which we can see more clearly by thinking about the sun for a moment, and in a way that is true of nothing else in creation. Glory, for instance. Fire, and the fear it produces. Otherness. The mysterious combination of great distance and felt presence, transcendence and immanence. The all-seeing, all-illuminating orbit, bringing heat and revelation to the entire world (Ps. 19:4–6). The fact that the sun is always shining, even when its light is concealed from us by the position of the earth or the covering of the clouds. Radiant brightness. Sheer power. When the apostles want us to see the splendor of Christ, sunshine is the only metaphor they need. "He was transfigured before them, and his face shone like the sun, and his clothes became white as light" (Matt. 17:2; see also Rev. 1:16).

The sun shows us something of the primacy, centrality, and sovereignty of God. It is a fountain of light: the first, the source, the origin of illumination for everything else. In ancient terms it is the "greater light" that rules the day, dictating the seasons, the days, the harvests, and the weather (Gen. 1:14–16). In modern terms it is the giant gravitational centerpiece of the solar system, containing 99.7 percent of the system's total mass and pulling everything else into its orbit. Although it is created, its existence even points to the independence of God, since the sun is a luminary in its own right rather than (like the moon) reflecting light from another source. It governs our notions of time (the hours of the day). It governs our notions of space (the points of the compass). Other than a human being, it is hard to think of anything in creation that highlights as many of God's characteristics as the sun.

There are subtler connections here as well. With the sun, as with God, there is no distinction between what it is and what it does. The sun gives light and heat because it is light and heat. Its action reflects its identity; its goodness is the overflow of its nature. And the same is true of God. He does good all the time because he is good all the time. "Every good gift and every perfect gift is from above, coming down from the Father of lights, with whom there is no variation or shadow due to change" (James 1:17). This may be why, when comparing God to the sun, the psalmist waxes lyrical about his goodness. "The LORD God is a sun and shield; the LORD bestows favor and honor. No good thing does he withhold from those who walk uprightly" (Ps. 84:11).[15]

For all these associations, however, the one that stirs my heart the most—and certainly the one that most of us sing about the most, at least in the English-speaking world—is the one that comes in Malachi 4. Malachi has no idea that he will be the last prophetic voice for more than four hundred years. He doesn't know that he is writing the final words of the Old Testament, at least in our English Bibles (the Hebrew Scriptures are ordered differently). But he wants God's people to know that no matter how long they have to wait, the Lord will surely come and judge evil and turn the hearts of the fathers to their children, and the children to their fathers. And he wants them not just to know but to feel the joy of that future moment, the joy of God's presence rising over them, even if they don't live to see it. "For you who fear my name," God promises, "the sun of righteousness shall rise with healing in its wings. You shall go out leaping like calves from the stall" (Mal. 4:2).

It is a beautiful image. The return of the King, when he comes, will prompt the kind of joy that a songbird feels at dawn or a photographer feels at sunrise. It will feel like the whole world is being healed by beams of celestial light. It will bring the abandon and gaiety that you see in newborn lambs and calves when they skip from their barns into spring fields in the morning, mingled with the relief experienced by emperor penguins when the sun finally breaks through at the end of an Antarctic winter. You will want to dance for joy because the long-awaited day of sunshine has come.

So every Christmas we sing about it and remind ourselves of the brightness that has broken into our darkness.

Hail, the heaven-born Prince of Peace!
Hail, the Sun of righteousness!
Light and life to all he brings
Risen with healing in his wings!

PART 2

NEW TESTAMENT

CHAPTER

16

SALT

THE PEOPLE OF GOD

*"You are the salt of the earth, but if salt has lost
its taste, how shall its saltiness be restored? It is no
longer good for anything except to be thrown out
and trampled under people's feet."*

—MATTHEW 5:13

Few things in creation are more ordinary than salt. Most of us
have interacted with it in the last couple of hours, whether we
realize it or not. We use it to make leather, pottery, soap, deter-
gents, rubber, clothes, paper, cleaning products, glass, plastics,
and pharmaceuticals. It sits largely unnoticed on hundreds of
millions of café and restaurant tables around the world. Unlike

pepper, which is often sitting next to it, salt is essential for our health and has always been eaten by human beings wherever we have settled. We add it to so much of our food that many languages simply distinguish between sweet and salty flavors. We spread it across the roads when it snows. More than half of the chemical products we make involve salt at some stage in the process. And that's without mentioning the trillions of tons of it that sit in our oceans, covering 70 percent of the surface of our planet. Salt is everywhere.

Its ordinariness and its use in all cultures make it an obvious candidate for Jesus to use as an illustration. Jesus, as we know, loved using everyday items to communicate truths about God and his people, and his description of the disciples as "the salt of the earth" (Matt. 5:13) is arguably the most famous example. To this day, people use the phrase to describe good, honest, humble people. Less predictably, it also features as the name of a Rolling Stones song, a D. H. Lawrence poem, and an intriguing variety of products including deodorants, water softeners, and (bafflingly) wine.

Here is the really odd thing, though: an awful lot of Jesus' disciples, the very people whom he identified as the salt of the earth, are still not entirely clear on what he meant. Lots of us have heard explanations of it—our job is to make the world taste better or stop it from rotting—but these explanations often conflict with each other and suffer from various problems. Jesus was talking about salt in relation to the earth, not food. Salting the earth was something people did after destroying their enemies, rather than blessing them. Elsewhere in the Gospels, Jesus connects salt with fire and with living at peace together (Mark 9:49–50), neither of which seem to fit with the idea of tastiness or preservation. Technically, sodium chloride doesn't lose its flavor anyway.[16] So what on earth is Jesus talking about?

The reason it is confusing is that salt had a number of purposes in the ancient world. At least five of them are relevant to Jesus' words about his disciples: salt was used for flavoring, preserving, sacrificing, destroying, and fertilizing. Rather than assuming that Jesus' statement is confusing and then debating which particular use of salt he had in mind, it is best to assume that he knew what he was doing and that (as we have seen throughout this book) metaphors can function in multiple ways at once. Followers of Jesus are like salt: although we are ordinary and everywhere and get involved in pretty much everything whether we are noticed or not, we also have a variety of roles to play as God's kingdom comes on earth. Let's consider each of those five purposes.

One: flavoring. Salt makes food taste better, either by adding flavor to something that would otherwise be bland (chips or fries), by enhancing flavors that are already there (vegetables), or by providing a contrast with a very different sort of taste (mmm, salted caramel). This is probably the use of salt that most of us think of, because it is the only one of the five that still applies today. Regardless of whether Jesus' original audience would also have thought of it first—and they may not have—it is a powerful illustration of the way Christians are to serve the world. We are intended to spread throughout the world and enhance it, adding flavor to things which would be bland, drawing out the blessings of whatever is good, and providing a contrast by being distinct and different. When Paul tells us to ensure that our speech is "seasoned with salt, so that you may know how you ought to answer each person" (Col. 4:6), this is the kind of thing he has in mind.

Two: preserving. Salt was the ancient equivalent of refrigeration. If you wanted to stop meat or fish from decaying, you could rub in salt and make it edible for longer. This was the main reason why salt was so valuable. Roman soldiers were sometimes paid in salt, which (as an interesting but thoroughly irrelevant aside) is the origin of our word salary. Disciples of Jesus, in this sense, are sent into the world to keep it from decay, preserving its goodness and preventing it from becoming corrupted or ruined, which is a helpful thing to bear in mind as we go to work every day. Salt does not just savor. It saves.

Three: sacrificing. This may well be related to the previous two functions of salt, although it is probably less familiar to us. Early in Israel's history, Moses explained how Israel was to offer sacrifices to the Lord: "You shall season all your grain offerings with salt. You shall not let the salt of the covenant with your God be missing from your grain offering; with all your offerings you shall offer salt" (Lev. 2:13). Perhaps because it flavored food and kept meat from going bad, salt was a necessary part of all of Israel's sacrifices and even represented God's covenant with them. "Disciples are salt in this sense, too," writes Peter Leithart. "The world is an altar. Humanity and the world are to become a single great offering to God. As we offer ourselves in obedient, suffering self-sacrifice, we become the seasoning on a cosmic sacrifice that makes it well-pleasing to God."[17]

Four: destroying. This is one we find much less appealing, but we can't get away from it: there are more scriptural references to salt being used in judgment or destruction than to any of the other purposes. When Lot's wife turns back to look at the city of Sodom, she is turned into a pillar of salt (Gen. 19:26), a story which Jesus refers to when describing the day of his coming

(Luke 17:32). Moses warns Israel that if they break God's covenant, their land will be "burned out with brimstone and salt, nothing sown and nothing growing, where no plant can sprout" (Deut. 29:23). When Gideon's son Abimelech tries to set himself up as king of Israel, the men of Shechem rebel against him, and he responds by razing the city and sowing it with salt (Judg. 9:45). The psalmist describes God turning "a fruitful land into a salty waste, because of the evil of its inhabitants" (Ps. 107:34). Jesus himself, in one of the fiercest judgment paragraphs in the Gospels, says simply that "everyone will be salted with fire" (Mark 9:49). Salt, in the ancient Near East, was used to express judgment upon evil.

There is a sense in which disciples have the same purpose. God scatters salty Christians into the world as a way of judging evil, destroying wickedness, and preventing lust or greed or murder or injustice from taking root. The very existence of the church, preaching and living out the gospel, proclaims judgment against the enemies of God and serves as what Paul calls "a clear sign to them of their destruction" (Phil. 1:28); this may be why Jesus says we are the salt of the earth immediately after describing the persecution we will face if we follow him. Frequently, of course, the church has failed to live this way and has been an accelerator of worldly evil, not a brake. But Jesus knew that would happen. That's why almost all his words of judgment are directed to the people of God rather than the unbelieving world. We need to be salted too.

Five: fertilizing. Several ancient civilizations used salt as a fertilizer for the soil, and depending on the conditions, it could help the earth retain water, make fields easier to plow, release minerals for plants, kill weeds, protect crops from disease, stimulate growth, and increase yields. The reason this matters is that Jesus specifically describes his people as the salt of the *earth*, which in a rural, farming culture would have been significant. Disciples are fertilizers. We are meant to be in those places where conditions are challenging and life is hard. We are sent to enrich the soil, kill weeds, protect against disease, and stimulate growth, and as we scatter, life springs up in unexpected places. Barren lands become fruitful. When the people of God are redeemed, as the prophet says, "the wilderness and the dry land shall be glad; the desert shall rejoice and blossom like the crocus" (Isa. 35:1).

So when Jesus said we are the salt of the earth, what did he mean? Did he mean that God will use us for flavoring, preserving, sacrificing, destroying, or fertilizing? In a word, yes. If anyone tells you that it is about only one of those things, by all means hear them out. But take it with a pinch of salt.

CHAPTER
17

RAIN

THE GRACE OF GOD

"Love your enemies and pray for those who
persecute you, so that you may be sons of your
Father who is in heaven. For he makes his sun rise
on the evil and on the good, and sends rain on the
just and on the unjust."

—MATTHEW 5:44–45

My drive into work is among the most beautiful in the world. From the moment you take the A267 at Hailsham, right up until you join the dual carriageway toward London on the far side of Tunbridge Wells, you meander through a twenty-five-mile stretch of avenue lined on both sides with deciduous

111

trees of deep green and liberally festooned with impossibly pink rhododendrons and azaleas. The villages are evocatively named: Horsebridge, Cross-in-Hand, Five Ashes, Mayfield, Mark Cross. Oast houses abound. So do bluebells on the forest floor, and village greens, timber-fronted pubs, houses with grand names and long driveways, and farms that sell logs, eggs, or cherries. Occasionally there is a break in the woodland, and you are surprised to find that you can see for miles, with nothing but undulating fields and hedges until the next church's bell tower. When you drive it in June, the color palette is so vivid, it's hard to believe.

There is something profligate about the way God has distributed beauty in the world. So far as I know, the people of the Sussex High Weald are not unusually godly, loving, or generous. The houses I drive past are just as likely to contain adultery or domestic violence, drug abuse or racism, as any others in the country. The expensive properties may be owned by people who work hard, pursue justice, love their neighbors, and give to the poor, or they may be owned by complete scoundrels who hoard wealth, exploit the weak, cheat on their taxes, and cheat on their partners. Yet God makes the sun rise and the rain fall on them just the same. They don't deserve to live in an Area of Outstanding Natural Beauty any more than I do. The beauty comes because of the sun and the rain, and the sun and the rain come because of grace.

It hits me every time I land at Gatwick Airport. When I look out of the airplane window as we circle around Sussex, waiting to land, it strikes me again how lush England is, in contrast to wherever I have just come from. (My wife, Rachel, finds it very tiresome that she cannot get through a simple descent without my "look how green it is" speech.) Often I am returning from a nation whose believers are far more numerous, joyful, humble, and prayerful than I am and whose governments have invaded and colonized far fewer countries than mine has. If rain were allocated on the basis of righteousness, then many of my brothers and sisters should be living in a verdant paradise and many of us should be living in an arid dust bowl. But it isn't, so we aren't. "He makes his sun rise on the evil and on the good, and sends rain on the just and on the unjust" (Matt. 5:45).

On my commute a few days ago, I was thinking about all this while listening to my playlist, and it occurred to me how exactly the same thing is true of human abilities. I get to marvel at a wide range of enormously talented people on my journey: Lin-Manuel Miranda, Sting, Rihanna, Eva Cassidy, Kurt Cobain, Madonna, Prince, Adele, Nina Simone, Frank Sinatra. I don't know any of them personally, and I hear that some of them are (or were) absolutely charming. But some of them are (or were) plagued by arrogance, greed, infidelity, bullying, smugness, anger, abusive behavior, and who knows what else. Apparently, there is no correspondence at all between the quality of someone's character and how gifted they are, hence the plots of movies like *Amadeus*, *The Social Network*, *Steve Jobs*, and numerous sporting films. If we were to discover that Shakespeare was a murderer, it would not make his plays any less brilliant (even if it made us less keen to perform them). Michael Jackson and Kevin Spacey do not become any less magnetic on-screen when their behavior off-screen is exposed. It feels unfair somehow. Talent, like rain, is showered on the evil as much as on the good.

The church has historically called this "common grace," and it is one of the great scandals of Christian theology. If I were God,

I would allocate ability according to merit: good people would be gifted, bad people would not be, and an increase in righteousness would earn an increase in talent. In my world, all the most gifted artists, intellectuals, musicians, and writers would be Christians, culture would be entirely shaped by honorable people, and Nobel Prize short lists and Oscar ceremonies would be populated by the ranks of the selfless. It would be a world of fairness, scrupulous evenhandedness, and ultimately—as uncomfortable as it might be to admit it—legalism.

God is different. He is a bountiful Father who lavishes excessive goodness on his creatures whether they like it (or him) or not. He scatters gifts like sunshine, and grace like rain. Nobody gets what they deserve, and it's just as well, or none of us would be here at all. This world is not set up to reward the righteous with nice weather, good looks, and quick minds; it is set up to proclaim the abundant goodness of the God revealed in Jesus, who loves his enemies and prays for those who persecute him. If you love and pray for your enemies, Jesus says, then you will take on the family likeness. You will be sons and daughters of your sunshine-giving, rain-pouring, grace-raining heavenly Father.

God's gracious gift of rain is the surprising punch line of the shortest and oddest evangelistic sermon in the New Testament. Barnabas and Paul are in Lystra, in modern-day Turkey, and they heal a man who has never been able to walk, which convinces the crowd that they are gods in human form. Horrified at the misunderstanding, they tear their clothes and plead with the town to turn from idols toward the living God. "In past generations he allowed all the nations to walk in their own ways," they explain. "Yet he did not leave himself without witness, for he did good by giving you rains from heaven and fruitful seasons, satisfying your hearts with food and gladness" (Acts 14:16–17). End of sermon. Even with this, Luke says, they barely stopped people from sacrificing to them.

The first dozen times I read that story, it made no sense to me. How could Paul, of all people, preach a message like that? You should turn to the living God because of *rain*? What is he playing at? But the more I think about it, the more appropriate it becomes. No doubt this is a short summary of what they said, and they may have explained the Jesus story in far more detail off camera. But when meeting pagans for the first time—pagans whose concept of deity is based on Zeus, whose temple and priest are central in their community (v. 13)—the apostles' first priority is to preach the goodness and benevolence of God. The Creator of all things is not like Zeus, they say. He is not a petty, vindictive, tit-for-tat, irascible tyrant who scratches your back only when you scratch his. He is a God who gives good gifts to everyone— rain, sunshine, fruit, harvests—whether they worship him or not. "The LORD is good to all, and his mercy is over all that he has made. . . . The eyes of all look to you, and you give them their food in due season" (Ps. 145:9, 15). Jerusalem serves Yahweh and Lystra serves Zeus, yet they both get rain from the same sky. We call it common grace because it is plentiful, but theologically speaking, it is as rare as they come.

As a natural legalist, I find grace difficult. The concept of just deserts runs deep in me, and I struggle to get my head around unmerited, incongruous favor. You may too. If so, then the next time you see dark clouds gathering overhead, stand outside and wait for the rainfall. Every droplet of water that splashes onto you or onto me is preaching to us that no matter how ungodly we are, our heavenly Father will continue to drench us with grace like rain. He does not divert the water toward only those individuals or nations who have reached a sufficient standard of justice; he pelts it over us indiscriminately, soaking us with his kindness, whatever sort of life we've led, gods we've worshiped, or day we've had. Stand there for a few minutes, and soak in the unmerited and unilateral goodness of God. You may even find yourself singing in the rain.

SEA

THE AWE OF GOD

They were filled with great fear and said to one another, "Who then is this, that even the wind and the sea obey him?"

—MARK 4:41

You never forget your first storm at sea.

I was a teenager, on holiday with my family, and we were returning from Denmark in a passenger ship. At some point in the late afternoon, the normal rocking motion of the liner became amplified, and over the course of a couple of hours the ship turned into a seesaw. My brothers and sisters and I found our way up to the cabins on B deck, where the rocking (we convinced ourselves) was at its most intense, and started playing a chasing game up and down the corridors while desperately trying to retain our footing as the floor disappeared beneath us. We persuaded our parents to let us go outside and were the last people to succeed before the crew closed the exits for safety reasons; my sister thought we were all going to die and remained inside with my mother, while the rest of us battled up the outside staircase in the rainy darkness, accompanied by howling winds and with my father holding on to my youngest brother's ankles to stop him from being blown overboard. The ship lurched backward and forward. We screamed with a mixture of terror and delight. By the time we reached A deck, we were eighty feet above sea level, but the waves were so fierce that it felt like someone was firing water cannons at the huge perspex screen in front of us. Only at breakfast the next morning did we discover how severe the storm had been; North Sea oil rigs had been blown adrift by it, and the captain had dropped anchor for seventeen hours because the engines were powerless against it. We arrived in Harwich an entire day late but with a newfound respect for the sea. If a five-hundred-foot ferry gets tossed around like that, we thought, imagine being in a clipper or a fishing trawler.

I often look back to that storm when I'm reading the Scriptures. The people of Israel were terrified of the ocean, as you can see in all kinds of biblical passages, and my North Sea experience helps me understand why. For many nations in the ancient world, the seas were a place of confusion and darkness: hundreds of miles of blank, featureless depths filled with monsters, storms, and marauding enemies. Israelites who sailed into the Mediterranean, often simply called the Great Sea, frequently got lost, shipwrecked, or killed or returned with stories of mysterious giants in the deep or got swallowed by a huge fish for three days or simply disappeared. Even today, with our engines, navies, and navigation systems, the open ocean has the capacity to frighten us with its unpredictability and scale, so you can hardly blame the Israelites for fearing it. (I love the ocean episode of *Planet Earth*, the BBC's outstanding nature program, which basically consists of David Attenborough pointing at weird things in the darkness for an hour and saying, "Yep, we have no idea what that is." Or I think of Harold Holt, the Australian prime minister who, even more bizarrely, went for a swim near Melbourne on December 17, 1967, and vanished without trace.) The sea can be scary.

Israel's view of the sea was not just practical, though. It was theological. The waters were often an agent of judgment, from which God's people needed to be rescued. In the beginning the earth was formless and void, shrouded in darkness and covered with water (Gen. 1:2), and life was possible only when God separated the waters and made dry land appear. When God judged humanity in Genesis, he effectively reversed this process, flooding the known world and washing away evil with it. The first attempt to exterminate the Hebrews was by drowning their boys in the waters of the Nile. When Israel eventually escaped, it was through the Red Sea, with Pharaoh's chariots buried in the ocean behind them. Jonah's fishy experience was not a nautical accident but a result of divine judgment. The sea, in the Old Testament, was spiritually significant as well as physically dangerous.

But Yahweh is King of the sea. So although the oceans could be frightening, Israel worshiped the God who created them, who made a boundary line for them that they could not cross (Ps. 104:9) and said to them, "Thus far shall you come, and no farther, and here shall your proud waves be stayed" (Job 38:11). The tide cannot advance an inch beyond the line set by its Creator. God is our refuge and strength, so we need not fear even when the oceans roar, foam, and swallow the mountains (Ps. 46:1–3). The sea is thunderous and powerful, but it pales in comparison with One who measures the waters in the hollow of his hand (Isa. 40:12). "Mightier than the thunders of many waters, mightier than the waves of the sea, the LORD on high is mighty!" (Ps. 93:4).

God's sovereignty over the sea gave great confidence to Israel in times of need. After all, Noah had been rescued through the flood, Moses had been rescued from the Nile, and Israel had been rescued from the Red Sea. On the basis of this track record of marine rescue, when Israel was facing exile and judgment centuries later, she could appeal to God to save her again. "Awake, awake, put on strength, O arm of the LORD; awake, as in days of old, the generations of long ago. Was it not you who cut Rahab in pieces, who pierced the dragon? Was it not you who dried up the sea, the waters of the great deep, who made the depths of the sea a way for the redeemed to pass over?" (Isa. 51:9–10). Wake up, O God! Save us from the waters of judgment, like you did before!

That brings a whole new meaning to the calming of the storm on the Sea of Galilee in Mark 4. ("Sea" is an interesting name for it, actually. Luke, the gentile, calls it the Lake of Gennesaret, which is fair enough, considering that it contains fresh water and is less than ten miles across. Matthew, Mark, and John, all Jews, call it the Sea of Galilee. They are saying, among other things, that this is a place of danger and confusion.) A storm strikes, the boat is lurching up and down, waves are crashing over the side, and the boat is at risk of sinking. Jesus meanwhile is asleep. So when they wake him up and cry for help, the echoes of Isaiah 51 are unmistakable. Wake up, O God! Save us from the waters of judgment, like you did before!

Jesus stands and rebukes the sea. "Peace! Be still!" (Mark 4:39). Instantly the water becomes calm, and the howling of the wind and the howling of the disciples are silenced. But notice: the famous line which follows—"Who then is this, that even the wind and the sea obey him?" (v. 41)—is not merely an expression of amazement that a powerful miracle has occurred. By this point in the gospel, the disciples have already seen plenty of those. It is the realization that there is only one King of the sea, one with the authority to say, "Thus far and no farther," one who can wake up to part the waters and still the waves and make a way for the redeemed to pass over. The disciples had left that evening on an eight-mile crossing with a sleepy rabbi, and they found themselves a few hours later in the middle of Isaiah 51 with the Creator of the world, the God of the exodus, the King of the sea. Who then is this?

While the storm was raging, they were afraid. But when it stopped and they realized who Jesus really was, they were filled with great fear. The sea was frightening, but the King of the sea was terrifying. The enemy induces fear, but not as much fear as the one who can destroy the enemy with a single word. In a strange twist, the disciples are more fearful at the end of the story than they were at the beginning.

But their fear is now in the one who is for them rather than against them. The fear of God always works like that. There is a sense in which Aslan is scarier than the White Witch, and Dumbledore more alarming than Voldemort. When you watch the final scene of *Jurassic Park*, you are more afraid of the T-Rex who comes to rescue the children than the velociraptors who are trying to kill them. When Simba and Nala are rescued from the elephant graveyard, they are more afraid of Mufasa (who is on their side) than of the hyenas (who are definitely not). But they are scared in a good way, because they know that he is on their side. It is not a cowering terror but an appreciative and reverent awe. And that is the only suitable response to the King of the sea.

From that point onward, something shifts in the story of Scripture and the sea. Two chapters later the disciples are in nautical trouble again, and Jesus walks toward them on the sea and says, "Take heart; it is I. Do not be afraid" (Mark 6:50) before once again silencing the wind and the waves. (We could translate it differently: "Take heart; I AM. Do not be afraid."[18]) In the book of Acts, we find the story of Jonah undone: another Jewish preacher heads west into the Mediterranean, but he is going to reach the gentiles rather than to avoid them, the sea becomes a means of transport rather than a means of judgment, and his shipwreck story ends with the entire crew being saved and the entire island of Malta being healed. The sea is still mighty, but one mightier has now come, and the turbulent ocean has been subdued.

Finally, when the new creation is described, there is water everywhere—a fresh, crystal-like, life-giving water that pours forth from the throne of God—but the writhing deep, the primal source of darkness and monsters, fear and confusion, has been abolished forever by the King of the sea. "Then I saw a new heaven and a new earth, for the first heaven and the first earth had passed away, and the sea was no more" (Rev. 21:1).

CHAPTER
19

FLOWERS

THE PROVISION OF GOD

"Consider the lilies, how they grow: they neither
toil nor spin, yet I tell you, even Solomon in all
his glory was not arrayed like one of these. But if
God so clothes the grass, which is alive in the field
today, and tomorrow is thrown into the oven, how
much more will he clothe you, O you of little faith!"

—LUKE 12:27–28

I get anxious sometimes, I tell him. He says, consider the lilies. So I do.

I buy a bouquet of them and put them in my kitchen and stare at them. The brightness of the white against the green, like clouds drifting over hilltops on a sunny day, makes it feel like spring even though it's October and it has been raining for two weeks solid. The fragrance fills the room, mingling with the smells of Fairy dishwashing liquid and burnt toast. Lilies have an aroma that is both startling and strangely familiar: startling because it is so fiercely sweet, as if their nectar is summoning me and not just the bees, but strangely familiar because it has been imitated (poorly) by everyone who has ever manufactured air freshener or fabric softener. A few days pass. Their splendor remains, but I have to fight to keep noticing them, and even more to keep considering them. Within a week they are starting to fade, and after ten days they are turning brown and have to be thrown away. I put them in the garden waste rather than the oven, but I don't think Jesus will mind.

Consider the lilies, he says. Think about them. Stare at them. Smell them. Get their pollen on your shirt if needed. Now, what do you notice? They don't do much, do they? They just sit there, unstressed and unhurried, without toiling or spinning. Their beauty is incomparable, but it isn't earned, it is given. They don't even last very long. Eventually you chuck them out and replace them with another bunch. Yet no human in history has been clothed like this. If God dresses them like that, as temporary and disposable as they are, then he'll dress you too. So why are you anxious?

Because I don't just want enough to wear, I reply. I don't just want enough to eat and a roof over my head. I want nice clothes and food I enjoy and plenty of personal space, and I don't know whether I am going to get them all. I want people to like me. I want my life to have meaning. I want my wife to be happy and my children to thrive and next week's meeting to go well and my reputation to be better tomorrow than it was yesterday. I want the lines in my finances to go up rather than down. I want to finish my life knowing that I have done enough, provided enough, loved enough. I want to live and not die. I want a myriad of things that may or may not happen. That's why I'm anxious. Is there any wisdom, any therapy you can suggest, for someone like that?

He says, flowers.

Consider the bluebells, he says. For eleven months of the year, they do nothing at all. They lie dormant in the woods, deep beneath the soil, hidden under an unglamorous canopy of fallen leaves and slowly rotting bracken. They are surrounded by trees, which tower over them and get to experience light every day. But they aren't worried by that. They bide their time. They know that when May finally arrives, they will all come out to play together, forming an elaborate carpet of deep blue that will summon townsfolk from miles around just to amble among them and get their children to pose for photos. They are not perennials, and they know it. They don't try to be something they're not. They take the water and nutrients that God gives, they grow in obscurity for much of the year, and when the seasons turn and the sun comes out, they rejoice.

Consider the roses, he says. They are a byword for love, even though dozens of flowers are at least as beautiful (orchids? dahlias? gerberas?), and dozens are at least as fragrant (it's hard to beat a daffodil in springtime, isn't it?). So why do they make so many appearances on Valentine's Day or at weddings? Because for all sorts of poetic and historical reasons, they have come to embody romance. A bunch of roses says, "I love you" far more than a bunch of wild daisies or crocuses, no matter how pretty the daisies or how scented the crocuses. So the true power of roses comes not from what they are in themselves—their pollen, the curvature of their petals, their color—but from what they represent. The meaning and value of the gift derives from the love of the giver. And if that is true of a rose, how much more is it true of a human being?

Consider the sweet peas, he says. They don't aspire to be more than they are. They don't look over their shoulder at the sunflowers and wonder why they aren't taller or brighter and yellower or more capable of being made into oil or allowed to live in the South of France or made with large black faces and strong stalks. They don't see their value in relative terms at all. They have been given delicate textures and gently blended purple and white petals, and they wear them with pride. They're much happier that way.

Consider the jade vine, he says. Some might think it an unsuccessful species. You've never heard of it, because it lives only in the rainforests of the Philippines, and it is almost impossible to grow anywhere else because it is pollinated mainly by bats. Bats! By most worldly metrics, it loses out to every other flower you can think of. But I love it. I delight in its minty green color and its hanging clusters of claw-like flowers. I love that the blooms look like butterflies with their wings folded and that for all its floral beauty, it is actually a bean. And I love that it carries on flowering in oddness and obscurity, unnoticed and unheralded, and doesn't care whether anyone has heard of it, content simply to be known and loved by me. Haven't I chosen the foolish things in the world to shame the wise?

Consider the dandelions, he says. It is hard to think of anything more fragile than a blowball. If any species has a right to be anxious, it would be a pale ball of fluff that can be blown to smithereens by a small child, carried by the wind, and scattered over a wide area. But then it takes root and becomes one of the most robust flowers anywhere, almost impossible to pull up with your bare hands, so much so that many exasperated gardeners call it a weed, and the French call it *dent de lion*, or "lion's tooth." Do you see? Its weakness is its strength. By giving itself up to be blown away, it rises indestructible and brings forth much fruit. If God so resurrects the dandelion, which is here today and gone tomorrow, will he not much more resurrect you, O you of little faith?

I still get anxious sometimes. I have noticed some patterns: my level of anxiety tends to be higher when I spend a lot of time with screens or money, and lower when I spend a lot of time with trees or children, although even the most serene moment can be gate-crashed by an unforeseen worry. But when that happens, I can speak to myself. I can tell my soul that my reasons for anxiety—comparison, ambition, fear of death, envy, distraction, dissatisfaction, or whatever it is—are far less compelling than they appear. I can say it with the help of the psalmist: "O Lord, my heart is not lifted up; my eyes are not raised too high; I do not occupy myself with things too great and too marvelous for me. But I have calmed and quieted my soul, like a weaned child with its mother" (Ps. 131:1–2). I can say it with Augustine: "You made us for yourself, O Lord, and our hearts are restless until they find their rest in you."[19] Or I can say it with flowers.

20

WIND

THE SPIRIT OF GOD

*"The wind blows where it wishes, and you hear its
sound, but you do not know where it comes from
or where it goes. So it is with everyone who is born
of the Spirit."*

—JOHN 3:8

Sometimes the wisdom of biblical imagery blows me away. Let's say you are trying to come up with a metaphor for the way that God works in the world, and it has to be one that could be grasped by a child. You need a simple, everyday image that communicates sovereignty without fatalism: an immense power that can do whatever it wants in absolute freedom but without destroying the meaningful response of other beings. The picture needs to show how God brings life to his creatures in creating them and continues to animate their daily lives on an ongoing basis. It needs to show how the Scriptures are divine in their content but also thoroughly human, without making the human authors either freewheeling innovators or reactive puppets. And if your metaphor could also find a way of explaining that God is spirit and therefore both invisible and immaterial without being any less real, that would be a bonus.

Your choice of metaphor has profound implications. Get it wrong, and you might set the church off course for the next two thousand years. If you picture the world like a machine and God as the master designer, as a number of people did in the eighteenth century, then you will create all sorts of unintended problems for people farther down the track. People will start describing the relationship between God and creation using words like watchmaker or engineer, and then terms like robot, automaton, programmed, process, system, and blueprint will creep into practical theology. Before you know it, both human freedom (to make meaningful choices) and divine freedom (to do anything other than watch things unfold) will have gone down the drain, and it will be your fault. With all that in mind, which image would you use? It's not easy, is it?

This is the genius of Scripture: not just that there is such an image and that every child from the age of about three can understand it but also that it is introduced in the second verse of the Bible. "In the beginning, God created the heavens and the earth. The earth was without form and void, and darkness was over the face of the deep. And the [Spirit-wind-breath] of God was hovering over the face of the waters" (Gen. 1:1–2). There you have it. Picture the activity of God in creation like a mighty wind preparing to blow across the face of the deep or like the breath of God preparing to animate and give life to his creatures.

To be fair, you can cheat if you're writing in Hebrew or Greek. In English, we have three words here: breath, from the Old English *braet*, meaning "scent"; spirit, from the Latin *spiritus*, meaning "breath" or "spirit"; and wind, from the German *Wind*, meaning . . . "wind." But the Hebrew word *ruach* covers all three of these meanings. So does the Greek word *pneuma*. In a single word, the writers of Scripture are able to hint at spirituality, invisible power, and life-giving breath, all at once.

For anyone who is a parent, this is an enormous help. Children are not very old when they start asking questions like, "Where is God?" and, "Why can't I see him?" In response, most of us have to look no farther than Jesus' explanation in John 3: you can't see the wind either as it picks up those leaves and swirls them around in circles, but you still know it's there, and you can still experience it for yourself. As they get older, we might graduate to John 4. God is spirit—like the wind, he doesn't have a body or physical limits or parts and he cannot be seen—and he wants people to worship him in spirit and truth (John 4:24).

If anything, the picture becomes even more useful as we mature. The language of Spirit-wind-breath is invaluable when we start asking questions about the sovereignty of God and the free choices of human beings. You might think that God's activity and ours are like the two ends of a seesaw: the more he does, the less there is for us to do. Lots of people think about it like that and then get flummoxed when they find the Bible talking as if the seesaw were down at both ends. But the relationship between divine and human activity isn't at all like a seesaw. It is more like what happens when you blow up a balloon: the more work you do, the more breath goes into the balloon, and therefore the more work there is for the latex to do. Or think of a child flying a kite: when a gust of wind comes, the child has to put in more effort than they had been previously, not less. The power does not come from us, nor are we passively letting things just happen to us. We work because he works (Phil. 2:12–13).[20] Like the wind.

A similar picture comes in useful with the doctrine of Scripture. How do we explain the idea that Scripture is God's word in human words? How do we do justice to both its divine author and its human authors without making it sound either like a figment of human imagination, with all the limitations, errors, and bias that implies, or like a mechanically dictated bit of text that falls leather-bound from the sky, complete with maps and blissfully unstained by the culture, language, personality, or history of the writers? Again, we do it by taking a page out of the apostles' books and using the image of the Spirit-wind-breath. All Scripture is *theopneustos*, says Paul (2 Tim. 3:16): the result of the breath, the wind, the spirit of God (hence our word inspiration). "Men spoke from God as they were carried along by the Holy Spirit," says Peter (2 Peter 1:21). Humans spoke with the breath God gave them. It's a powerful picture.

Think about a talented jazz musician like Miles Davis. He can play a variety of instruments—trumpet, flugelhorn, saxophone, clarinet, or whatever—and they all make different sounds, according to the kind of music he is playing. When he blows into each one, he is putting his breath into the instrument, and he is the one responsible for ensuring it is played perfectly: he chooses the instrument, plays the note as high, low, long, or short as he wants it, and is the one who (rightly) receives praise for the quality of the performance. But the shapes, moods, textures, and flavors of the sounds made by each instrument are different, reflecting the way they have been made. The same breath that makes a trumpet bold can make a saxophone sultry and a clarinet wistful. The same Spirit-wind-breath can speak through Jeremiah and Moses, Paul and John, and produce very different sounds, colored by all the richness of their human experience. But the words have still been breathed out by God.

Perhaps the most powerful application of the Spirit-wind-breath image, in my experience, relates to our experience of God in everyday life. When Paul tells us to "be filled with the Spirit" (Eph. 5:18), for example, it can sound rather strange. How on earth do you obey a passive verb? Clearly, I can obey an active verb (like "Phone your mother"), and we all do that all the time. But what are we supposed to do if someone says, "Be phoned by your mother"? It can be confusing.

As a result, a lot of Christians aren't entirely sure what being filled with the Spirit is. Is it an experience we are supposed to have, and if so, what? Is it a series of habits we are supposed to develop, and if so, which ones? Reformed and conservative believers will often emphasize the habit, based on the parallel instruction in Colossians to "let the word of Christ dwell in you richly" (3:16). Pentecostal and charismatic types will usually emphasize the experience and connect it to the baptism in the Spirit in the book of Acts. But when we read the metaphor in light of the Spirit-wind-breath, it instantly becomes much clearer. Particularly if you have ever been sailing.

Catching the wind on a sailing boat is clearly an experience—I vividly remember the first time it happened to me—in which you are seized and carried forward by a mighty power from elsewhere. You rely entirely on the external power to get you anywhere, and no sailor imagines themself to be powering the boat in their own strength. (You will know this if you've ever gone sailing after going rowing.) As Paul insists in Romans 7–8, being powered by muscle/flesh is utterly different from being powered by wind/Spirit.

At the same time, catching the wind is also a habit. If you don't put the sails up, pull the mainsheet fast, or adjust the jib, the wind may be blowing powerfully, but you won't go anywhere. You have to respond attentively to whatever the wind is doing, and that comes through awareness and skill and cultivating good habits. Sailing, in that sense, is the art of attentive responsiveness to an external power. The Spirit-wind-breath is mighty and powerful and brings life-changing experiences, but we are responsible for aligning ourselves with him and learning from him. "If we live by the Spirit, let us also keep in step with the Spirit" (Gal. 5:25).

God is Spirit—invisible, untamable, powerful, life-giving, and wild, yet without destroying our agency or personality—and following him is like sailing. Like kite flying. Like jazz. It's an adventure.

CHAPTER

21

WATER

THE LIFE OF GOD

Jesus said to her, "Everyone who drinks of this
water will be thirsty again, but whoever drinks of
the water that I will give him will never be thirsty
again. The water that I will give him will become
in him a spring of water welling up to eternal life."

—JOHN 4:13-14

Water is a wonder. You don't need me to tell you that. Life on earth is possible without many of the things in this book (honey, pigs, clothes, and so on) and would probably be much more pleasant for us without some of them (earthquakes, viruses). But water is essential. Every known life form requires water to survive, whether it needs a drink every few hours, like you, or can survive without one for a hundred years, like a tardigrade. (Google them. They're pretty weird.) Water is vital. It is not just important but necessary for anything to be alive.

It is a molecular marvel. Its specific heat capacity is the highest of any liquid, which basically means that it is harder to heat up or cool down than anything else, and this means that it acts as a giant temperature stabilizer, keeping the planet cool in summer and warm in winter. (If you live on an island, like I do, you get this benefit locally as well as globally, and that's something you feel smug about if you have friends in Chicago.)

I remember where I was, in Central London, when I heard a pastor from Nairobi explain the wisdom of God through the chemical properties of water. Every other substance you can think of, he said, is denser as a solid than as a liquid. That's what you learned in chemistry at school. When elements boil, they turn into gases and get more spread out; when they freeze, they turn into solids and get more condensed. So if you put solid gold into a pool of liquid gold, or solid hydrogen into a pool of liquid hydrogen, or whatever, the solid would sink. That's what happens with every substance you can think of and with every element that is liquid at room temperature.[21]

With one exception. When water boils and becomes steam, like every other liquid, it expands. But when it freezes and becomes ice, remarkably, it expands as well. Ice is about 9 percent larger than the same mass of water, which is the reason why icebergs are a thing, cans of beer explode if you leave them too long in the freezer, and ice cubes float in your Coke. All other liquids sink as they freeze. But for reasons of molecular chemistry that I don't really understand (and certainly couldn't explain), frozen water floats.

Consider the implications. We need water to expand when it boils, because if it didn't, it would sink instead of evaporating, and we wouldn't have clouds or rain or any fresh water anywhere (because all fresh water would eventually run into the sea and not be replaced), and we would all die. But we also need water to expand when it freezes. If it didn't, there would be no such thing as icebergs, which drift on the surface of the ocean, eventually receive the warmth of the sun, and melt. Instead, when the temperature got below a certain point, ice would sink to the seabed, receive no warmth from the sun, and gradually cause many of the oceans to freeze from the bottom up, and we would all die. So God created water with chemical properties that somehow, in ways that only very bright people have figured out very recently, cause it to expand both when it boils and when it freezes. "O LORD, how manifold are your works! In wisdom have you made them all" (Ps. 104:24).

For most of us, presumably, the wonder of water is found not in biology, physics, or chemistry but in the very ordinary ways in which we depend on it in our daily lives. We may not understand it or even think about it that much, but we know we need it, and for the exact same reasons that everyone in history has needed it: for drinking, for cleaning, and for farming. If we bear that in mind as we read the Scriptures, we will find something striking. In each of these three ways, our need for water mirrors our need for God, and in particular for the person of the Holy Spirit.

We are thirsty creatures. One of the first things we do in the morning is to have a drink, which is also virtually the first thing we do after we are born. Genuine thirst is something we rarely experience if we live in a country with safe drinking water, although if you have ever underestimated the heat of a day or the length of a hike, or both, you'll know the feeling: the cardboard mouth, the stick-like tongue, the thumping in your temples, the endless fantasies of encountering a river, a fountain, or even a fellow traveler who is more prepared than you are. Thirst, more than any other human experience, causes obsession: the realization that for all our strengths and abilities, we simply cannot live without water, and in the right circumstances we would do anything to get it.

That desperation is how David describes his intense need for the living God. "O God, you are my God; earnestly I seek you; my soul thirsts for you; my flesh faints for you, as in a dry and weary land where there is no water" (Ps. 63:1). It is a vivid, visceral image, one made more authentic by the fact that it was written by a man in hiding in the wilderness of Judah, and more powerful by the confession that follows it: "Because your steadfast love is better than life, my lips will praise you" (v. 3). I may be the anointed king, David is saying, and I may have commanded armies and slain giants. But I cannot live without you. Nothing else will satisfy me; I need you like a camel seeks an oasis, like a deer pants for a stream (Ps. 42:1–2), like Israel craved water from the rock (Ex. 17:1–7; Num. 20:1–13).

We, like David, are thirsty, desperate people, parched and helpless without our Creator. Our only hope comes from the loud shout of Jesus: "If anyone thirsts, let him come to me and drink. Whoever believes in me, as the Scripture has said, 'Out of his heart will flow rivers of living water'" (John 7:37–38). John immediately explains: "Now this he said about the Spirit, whom those who believed in him were to receive" (v. 39). Our spiritual thirst, as intense as it is, is deliciously quenched as we come to the Fountain of Life and drink deeply of his Spirit.

Just as we need water for drinking, we need water for cleaning. I wash all kinds of things in an average week—my teeth, body, hair, clothes, children, dishes, car, house—and every act of washing involves water. The natural state of things in a fallen world is that they decay, so I am in a continuous battle with dirt. But I have water on my side. Dust, sweat, grime, crumbs, even the mighty dried baked bean, have no defense against the cleansing power of H_2O.

This too is used by the apostles and prophets to picture the work of God's Spirit. He is the Spirit of cleansing, a pressure hose who washes away impurities and renews people into spotless, stainless beauty. Ezekiel, who speaks more luridly than anyone about the filth of God's people, describes the new covenant as a spiritual wash down. In the book of Ezekiel, God tells the prophet to say to the Israelites, "I will sprinkle clean water on you, and you shall be clean from all your uncleannesses. . . . And I will put my Spirit within you, and cause you to walk in my statutes and be careful to obey my rules" (36:25, 27). Jesus himself, drawing from Ezekiel, explains that you cannot enter the kingdom unless you are born of water and the Spirit (John 3:5), and John the Baptist describes Jesus as one who will baptize (drench, immerse, soak) his people in the Holy Spirit (Mark 1:8). Paul reminds us that we have been "washed . . . by the Spirit of our God" (1 Cor. 6:11) and saved "by the washing of regeneration and renewal of the Holy Spirit, whom [God] poured out on us richly through Jesus Christ our Savior" (Titus 3:5–6). The Holy Spirit is not just a thirst quencher but a dirt cleanser. He is water to our souls, in more ways than one.

And he is the rain. In most societies, when it finally rains after a long period of drought, people celebrate because now at last crops will grow and animals will feed. (England is an exception: it rains plenty, but we always seem to focus on how it is good for the garden.) Water is life-giving, not just in the chemical sense we saw earlier but in the very tangible way in which the rains transform the landscape from brown to green. In its absence nothing grows and all is dust. In its presence we find life, health, growth, abundance, freshness, and color.

So it is with the Spirit. "I will pour water on the thirsty land, and streams on the dry ground; I will pour my Spirit upon your offspring, and my blessing on your descendants" (Isa. 44:3). The Spirit comes like rain, drenching and saturating and pouring out over people, turning deserts into meadows and death into life. The Spirit comes like a river, surging and flowing and lining the riverbanks with fruit trees and overhanging willows. When the Spirit comes, "waters break forth in the wilderness, and streams in the desert; the burning sand shall become a pool, and the thirsty ground springs of water" (Isa. 35:6–7). The curse of barrenness turns into the blessing of abundance. The empty scrubland becomes a well-watered garden.

Water is vital. There would be no life without it. Its remarkable properties make our planet, like Goldilocks' porridge, not too hot and not too cold, and we depend on it daily to quench our thirst, cleanse our dirt, and grow our crops. Yet in each of these ways, water is a mere shadow of the Holy Spirit, the Lord and the giver of life, through whom all things are created, our world sustained, and our lives made possible, pure, and productive. "Everyone who drinks of this water will be thirsty again," Jesus explained to a puzzled woman as he sat next to a well in the heat of the day, "but whoever drinks of the water that I will give him will never be thirsty again. The water that I will give him will become in him a spring of water welling up to eternal life" (John 4:13–14).

CHAPTER 22

BREAD

THE SON OF GOD

*Jesus said to them, "I am the bread of life; whoever
comes to me shall not hunger, and whoever
believes in me shall never thirst."*

—JOHN 6:35

For the last ten thousand years, most human beings have gotten virtually all of their calories by eating one basic crop. The local staple varies from place to place; for most of our ancestors it was either a cereal of some kind (wheat, rice, maize, millet, sorghum) or a root vegetable (potato, yam, cassava, taro, sweet potato), but pretty much everyone has had one, with the exception of hunter-gatherers and supermarket shoppers. Villages, towns, cities, and even civilizations have been built around one staple. In most generations you could walk for days without meeting a single person who had not eaten the same basic breakfast, lunch, and dinner you had. The shape of the day and of the year was organized around the cultivation of one plant, in ways that still influence many cultures to this day (which is partly why children in rice societies spend far longer at school every year than children in wheat or potato societies, for example).[22] And you were utterly dependent on just one plant for your family to get by. If the harvest died, so did you. Mealtimes were a matter not of choice but of survival.

In Western Eurasia, including all the lands featured in the Bible, that crop was wheat: a tall grass with seeds at the top that can be harvested as grain, ground into flour, and then mixed with water and baked to make bread. It dominated people's diets, social lives, and annual calendars. When the first wheat crop came through, they celebrated with a festival; when the rest of the harvest arrived, they celebrated with another festival (Leviticus 23). Bread was the primary feature of every meal, to the extent that God could describe the hard work of farming as eating bread "by the sweat of your face" (Gen. 3:19), and a rich man like Abraham could describe killing a calf for his guests as bringing "a morsel of bread" (Gen. 18:5). In some ways the biblical word *bread* corresponds more closely to our concept of food than our concept of bread. It was not just an important part of a meal, or even the most popular one, but the essence of all meals. Bread was life.

It is hard to get our heads around that in our world of artisan loaves, supermarkets, and gluten-free diets. Because we are familiar with the word *bread*, we can assume we know what it represents when we come across it in the Scriptures. But in our world bread is optional. My friend Sam Allberry points out that when a waiter asks if we would like a bit of bread for the table, we might say no, seeing it as an appetizer before the real food comes out, and then we read that sort of take-it-or-leave-it approach into our Bibles. So when Jesus says, "I am the bread of life" (John 6:35), we respond as if he were offering us a bit of Jesus for the table, a spiritual appetizer before we get into the real business of working and socializing and shopping.[23] Ouch.

In the biblical world, on the other hand, bread is essential. It is life-giving, and without it you starve. So whereas we think it is fairly obvious that "man does not live by bread alone" (Deut. 8:3), and might even take it as a biblical invitation to a varied diet, the people of Israel would have thought the opposite. For them, the idea that human beings were more dependent on God's word than on bread, the essential food for everyone they had ever met, was so weird that it took forty years of coriander flake wafers miraculously falling out of the clear blue sky for them to get the message.

Because bread was so essential, it was also highly communal. In a world where you need bread for your family to survive, breaking bread with someone—tearing your loaf and giving a chunk of it to someone else—was a significant act of inclusion, even intimacy. Again, we often find this hard to understand. Many of us eat our daily bread in silence, hurriedly pulling triangular slices out of plastic packaging as we walk down the street or sit at our desks, alongside dozens of other people doing the same thing, with no sense of community whatsoever. But in ancient Israel, to break bread with a person was to welcome and accept them and to give them something very valuable. That's why the psalmist feels such betrayal when he is attacked by "my close friend in whom I trusted, who ate my bread" (Ps. 41:9). To invite someone to share in your loaf was to invite them to share in your family.

And because bread was essential and communal, eating it was a natural context for expressing gratitude and blessing to God. To tear a loaf of bread was to be reminded that God had provided for you once again, giving you the sun and rain and seed and growth that you needed to be able to feed your family. One of the most well-known Jewish prayers expresses this beautifully: "Blessed are you, Lord our God, Ruler of the universe, who brings forth bread from the earth." If you look carefully, you'll notice the same thing happening repeatedly in the New Testament, especially in the ministry of Jesus. As he prepares to feed the five thousand, Jesus takes the loaves, looks to heaven, and blesses God, and then he distributes more than enough for everyone (Matt. 14:19). At the Last Supper, he takes bread, gives thanks, and then breaks it and gives it to the disciples (Luke 22:19). Over dinner in Emmaus at the end of Easter Sunday, he does it again (Luke 24:30); apparently, it is such a familiar habit of his that the disciples instantly recognize him. Bread breaking is essential and communal, but it is also thankful, worshipful, grateful.

Hopefully, this gives us some idea of the depth and richness of Jesus' extraordinary statement in John 6: "I am the bread of life." It is not an appeal to taste. Jesus is not saying that he is a savory appetizer or a side dish or a popular choice among people who like their spirituality nutritional and fresh from the oven. He is claiming to be essential, life-giving, one upon whom human beings are entirely dependent and without whom we cannot function properly. He is claiming to be manna in person: the Son of God, the gift of God, come down from heaven to nourish people who would otherwise die of hunger. He is saying that our need for bread—which he is happy to provide for, having just fed five thousand people with a lunchbox (John 6:1–14)—pales in comparison with our need for him. If we have ears to hear, he is also hinting that those who "eat" him in faith will become united together in community around the same table and find in doing so the ultimate reason for gratitude toward and worship of the God who brings forth the Bread of Life to feed them. Jesus is essential, like bread, and he wants us to share in him communally and worshipfully.

All of these elements come together gloriously in the Lord's Supper. The broken body of Jesus is vital for us. Without him, and without his sacrificial death on our behalf, we die of spiritual hunger just as surely as we would without bread. We come to the Lord's Table as needy, empty, dependent creatures, desperately needing a meal from heaven to satisfy us and strengthen us for the days ahead—not worthy, as the Book of Common Prayer puts it, to gather up crumbs from under God's table but confident that he is forever the same Lord, whose nature is always to have mercy. He invites us and we come. He spreads the table and we feast. If we ask our Father for heavenly bread, he won't fob us off with a stone instead.

At the same time, we experience communion in the breaking of bread: participation with Christ and unity with one another, because we all share in one loaf (1 Cor. 10:16–17). As we break the bread Christ has given to us and then give it to one another, we make two profound statements of inclusion. The first is that Christ has included us and given us the right to share with him. The second is that on this basis we include one another, expressing fellowship, hospitality, and forgiveness in the communal meal. When I break bread with you, I am giving you (and receiving from you) something of immense value, the free sharing of which communicates love as tangibly as anything else. We welcome one another, as God in Christ has welcomed us.

And while both of these things are happening, we also join together in the Eucharist: the act of *eucharistia*, thanksgiving to God, for his unimaginable grace in providing exactly what we need. We receive the body of Jesus as a gift and bless God for giving him to us. We take the elements seriously but not gloomily; our worship is characterized by a spirit of thankfulness and joy, just as an ancient Israelite would give thanks to God for the gift of bread. Sins are forgiven! The new covenant is here! The body of Jesus has been broken for us at the cross and handed round the family to give us life! We feed on him in our hearts, by faith, with thanksgiving.

At the end of John 6, Jesus has made so many striking, exclusive, and shocking claims about himself that virtually everyone has left. The vast crowds who followed him, their bellies still full from the lavish dinner he had laid on the previous evening, have drifted away, his Judean debaters have taken offense, and even many of his disciples have abandoned him. As the chapter concludes, he asks the Twelve if they are going to leave him too. But Peter responds like a man who has grasped just how essential the Bread of Life really is. "Lord, to whom shall we go? You have the words of eternal life" (John 6:68).

Eat that.

TREES

THE CROSS OF GOD

*"The God of our fathers raised Jesus, whom you
killed by hanging him on a tree."*

—ACTS 5:30

The Bible starts with two trees and ends with one. In the beginning
there is the tree of life (representing obedience and righteousness) and the tree of the knowledge of good and evil (representing
independence, rebellion, and death). By the end only one remains:
"the tree of life with its twelve kinds of fruit, yielding its fruit each
month. The leaves of the tree [are] for the healing of the nations"
(Rev. 22:2). At some point in the story of Scripture, two have become
one, and what is mortal has been swallowed up by life.

It leads to the most curious image in the Bible's final chapter (which is full of curious images). John says the tree of life is "on either side of the river" (v. 2). But this makes no sense. You cannot have one tree on both sides of a river. At most you can have a tree on one bank which is so large that its foliage stretches across to the other, but this isn't what John says.

The image becomes even stranger when you realize that John has taken it from Ezekiel 47:12, in which (far more logically) there are numerous trees on both sides: "On the banks, on both sides of the river, there will grow all kinds of trees for food." Yet John, for some reason, has deliberately changed the picture into something that cannot physically happen: one tree on both sides of a river. In Genesis there were two trees, and in Ezekiel there were lots of them, but in the new creation there is only one. What on earth is going on?

I can think of only two explanations. Either John hasn't noticed that his description makes no sense, or he has concluded that the strangeness of the image is compensated for by the power of the symbolism: that in all the world there is one tree, and one tree only, whose fruit is bountiful enough to feed the world and whose leaves are sufficient to heal the nations. I think John has a tree in mind, and it is one that he encountered himself, staring at it for six terrible hours that must have seemed like months. The tree of Calvary.

If that sounds like a stretch, consider two things. First, in both Hebrew and Greek, the word *tree* does not mean just a living organism that has roots, branches, and leaves. It also refers to the thing that those living organisms are made of: wood. (The same was true of the English word *tree* five hundred years ago, as it happens.) Goliath the Gittite has a spear with a large *ets*

(2 Sam. 21:19), but this clearly doesn't mean he's throwing a tree. When the pantomime villain Haman decides to build an *ets* overnight in order to hang Mordecai (Est. 5:9–14), it's pretty obvious that he is building not a tree but a large wooden structure. In modern English, we make a sharp distinction between the substance (wood) and the organism (tree), but in the biblical languages they didn't, and this means that connections which look obscure to us would have looked much clearer to them.

Second, although there is a perfectly good Greek word for the cross (*stauros*), the apostles often talk instead about the tree (*xylos*). Given that the crucifixion of Jesus is at the heart of the Christian gospel, it is astonishing that the word *cross* does not appear once in the entire book of Acts. Rather the apostles proclaim that Jesus was killed "by hanging him on a tree" (5:30; 10:39) and that afterward "they took him down from the tree and laid him in a tomb" (13:29). Paul points out that Christ became a curse for us by being "hanged on a tree" (Gal. 3:13). Peter says that Jesus "bore our sins in his body on the tree" (1 Peter 2:24). Clearly, there is something about the crucifixion that is not just cross-like but tree-like.

Part of this is based on the Jewish law, which says that anyone who is hanged on a tree is cursed by God (Deut. 21:23). For Paul this is crucial, because it shows that by being crucified and literally hanging on a wooden structure, Christ was becoming a curse *for us*. He had done nothing which deserved death but was hanged on a tree anyway. So, since the law says that he was therefore cursed, he must have been taking our curse upon himself and freeing us from it in the process. In that sense the cross is a tree: a place where curses are borne and satisfied.

This cursedness is in turn related to the sense of exposure, degradation, and humiliation which comes from being hung on a tree for all to see. Methods of death that do this, whether by impaling, crucifying, or lynching, are designed to dehumanize the victim. Bodies are left hanging, often naked, sometimes for days. They decompose and get eaten by insects, in full public view. Onlookers can see the person's humanity appear to disintegrate in front of them. The whole process proclaims to the community, this is a nonperson. If you step out of line, you will become like this.

In that sense, as James Cone has argued, the cross can be seen as a lynching tree.[24] Jesus, like the five thousand black people lynched in the United States between 1880 and 1940, was scapegoated for the crime of another, stripped of his clothes in front of a mob baying for blood, shamed, humiliated, spat upon, disfigured, killed, and left to hang there as a warning to others, in order to reinforce the supremacy of a powerful group over a powerless one. His clothes, like the clothes (and sometimes the body parts) of lynching victims, were distributed as souvenirs for his killers. Such a connection between the ancient world and ours may make us uncomfortable—and it should!—but it may also help us to grasp the dehumanizing savagery of a very familiar moment. He himself bore our sins, in his body, on the tree.

So by talking about Jesus dying on a tree, the apostles help us connect all sorts of dots, both back in time to the giving of the Jewish law and forward in time to the twenty-first century. But they also draw out the point that John makes in Revelation 22. The biblical arboretum starts with two trees and ends with one.

Jesus is nailed to a tree of death—the cursed tree, the tree of the law which gives us the knowledge of good and evil—but by doing so in our place, he turns it into the tree of life. The tree which was designed to dehumanize and bring death now makes us more alive than we ever dreamed and more fully human than we ever hoped. So the cross is not dead wood. It is a living and life-giving tree, covered with leaves and festooned with fruit, and the fruit comes in twelve varieties every month, and the leaves are for the healing of the nations.

Every week, we invite people to come to the tree of life. Taste the fruit of friendship with God. Receive healing from him who has borne the curse for us. Eat and drink. And do this in remembrance of him.

CHAPTER
24

TRUMPETS

THE VICTORY OF GOD

Behold! I tell you a mystery. We shall not all sleep,
but we shall all be changed, in a moment, in the
twinkling of an eye, at the last trumpet. For the
trumpet will sound, and the dead will be raised
imperishable, and we shall be changed.

—1 CORINTHIANS 15:51–52

Musical instruments communicate more than we realize. We may not always be able to identify an instrument, but we will often be able to identify what feel, mood, atmosphere, even meaning it carries. Cellos sound haunting and wistful. Xylophones sound childlike or humorous. Bongos make us feel energized, and violas make us feel sad. If someone were to replace all the duduk music in *Gladiator* with harmonica music, it would become a different movie; tragic scenes would turn into irony-laden farce, even if the tune were unchanged. The same melody could make you feel like you were in three different places or even centuries, depending on whether it was played on a harpsichord (an eighteenth-century European ballroom), a tin whistle (medieval Scotland), or a flugelhorn (a 1930s club in New Orleans).

But the instrument that carries the most meaning throughout human history is surely the trumpet. In societies where musical options were much narrower than ours, trumpets could function like a dance track, an air-raid siren, a church organ, a twenty-one-gun salute, or a horror movie soundtrack, depending on the context. If we limit ourselves to the Scriptures, I count seven things that trumpets can mean, and when John describes a sequence of seven trumpets in Revelation or when Paul talks about the instant transformation which will take place at the last trumpet, that is worth bearing in mind.

One: trumpets are associated with fear. When Israel finally arrives at Mount Sinai, having been redeemed from Egypt and brought through the Red Sea, they are not sitting quietly on the desert floor, as you might guess from the final scene of *The Prince of Egypt*. They are terrified as the Lord descends on the mountain in fire and announces his arrival with the sound of the trumpet. "On the morning of the third day there were thunders and lightnings and a thick cloud on the mountain and a very loud trumpet blast, so that all the people in the camp trembled. . . . And as the sound of the trumpet grew louder and louder, Moses spoke, and God answered him in thunder" (Ex. 19:16, 19). The power of a trumpet blast to provoke fear is well known, which is why they have so often been used in warfare, but it is significant that the first time we encounter them in the Bible, they are not sounded by Israel to generate terror among her enemies but sounded by God to generate awe among his friends. It almost works too well. "Now when all the people saw the thunder and the flashes of lightning and the sound of the trumpet and the mountain smoking, the people were afraid and trembled, and they stood far off and said to Moses, 'You speak to us, and we will listen; but do not let God speak to us, lest we die'" (20:18–19). But notice how Moses responds. "Do not fear, for God has come to test you, that the fear of him may be before you, that you may not sin" (v. 20). The trumpet of God is supposed to make us bow in awe, not cower and withdraw.

Two: trumpets symbolize freedom and in particular for Jews, the Year of Jubilee. "Then you shall sound the loud trumpet on the tenth day of the seventh month. On the Day of Atonement you shall sound the trumpet throughout all your land. And you shall consecrate the fiftieth year, and proclaim liberty throughout the land to all its inhabitants. It shall be a jubilee for you" (Lev. 25:9–10). If the Sinai trumpet sounded like a thunderclap, the Jubilee trumpet sounds like a samba: a nationwide invitation to a party that brings people spilling out into the streets. It is a proclamation of release and liberty, and a particular cause for celebration among those who are enslaved, indebted, and trapped. For the hopeless and homeless, the blast of the Jubilee trumpet was the Bronze Age equivalent of Martin Luther King Jr.'s famous punch line: "Free at last! Free at last! Thank God Almighty, I'm free at last!"

Three: trumpets mean battle, serving as alarms that muster

the people to respond. They are ancient sirens, which are no sooner raised than people stop what they are doing, gather their weapons, and assemble in readiness for war. Sometimes they summon people to attack their oppressors. "When you go to war in your land against the adversary who oppresses you, then you shall sound an alarm with the trumpets, that you may be remembered before the LORD your God, and you shall be saved from your enemies" (Num. 10:9). Sometimes they call for defense. "In the place where you hear the sound of the trumpet, rally to us there. Our God will fight for us" (Neh. 4:20). But in both cases it is interesting that the battle trumpet not only musters the troops but also summons divine assistance; like the horn of Susan in Narnia and the horn of Gondor in *The Lord of the Rings*, it serves not just as an alarm but as a prayer. The battle belongs to the Lord.

Four: trumpets mean victory. This follows naturally from the previous meaning but goes dramatically beyond it. Trumpets were familiar in the ancient world as a way of gathering an army, beginning a march, and intimidating the enemy. But nobody thought that trumpets could win battles on their own. They were significant because of what they represented—soldiers and weapons, horses and chariots—not because they had any power in themselves. So you can imagine the astonishment of the Israelites (to say nothing of the Canaanites) when God told them that they would capture Jericho with nothing but trumpets and a shout. Nevertheless: "So the people shouted, and the trumpets were blown. As soon as the people heard the sound of the trumpet, the people shouted a great shout, and the wall fell down flat, so that the people went up into the city, every man straight before him, and they captured the city" (Josh. 6:20). Gideon pulled off a similar stunt a few decades later against equally improbable odds. "When they blew the 300 trumpets, the LORD set every man's sword against his comrade and against all the army" (Judg. 7:22). A God-given trumpet will conquer a man-made city or an army of men every time. "By you I can run against a troop, and by my God I can leap over a wall" (Ps. 18:29).

Five: trumpets can communicate peace, the cessation of hostilities between two armies, like the solemn firing of ceremonial cannons or the twenty-one-gun salute. (This might sound like it is in tension with the previous two points, but if you think about it, that's exactly how a whistle functions in many sports: it starts the match, ends the match, and declares victory.) This is what happens at the end of the battle of Gibeon, between the armies of David and the armies of Saul. "So Joab blew the trumpet, and all the men stopped and pursued Israel no more, nor did they fight anymore" (2 Sam. 2:28). The same thing happens after Absalom's rebellion. "Then Joab blew the trumpet, and the troops came back from pursuing Israel" (18:16). The war may have been lost or it may have been won, but the trumpet blast means it is over. Shalom is restored.

Six: trumpets are associated with kings, and in particular the moment when a new king replaces an old one. On several occasions in Scripture, a plot or a coup is foiled by the blowing of a trumpet and the announcement that people are loyal to the rightful king rather than the pretender to the throne. That is how David ensures that the kingdom passes to his son Solomon rather than Adonijah (1 Kings 1:34–49). It is how Jehu is proclaimed king in Israel (2 Kings 9:13) and how Athaliah realizes that her attempt to usurp the throne by assassinating Joash as a young boy has come unstuck (2 Chron. 23:13); her head comes unstuck soon afterward. Coronation trumpets strike fear into the hearts of rebels like Athaliah and Adonijah, unsurprisingly, but for all who support the rightful king they are a cause for celebration. "There was the king standing by the pillar, according to the custom, and the captains and the trumpeters beside the king, and all the people of the land rejoicing and blowing trumpets" (2 Kings 11:14). Trumpets enthrone the true king.

Seven: trumpets mean celebration. Israel was commanded to blow trumpets "on the day of your gladness" (Num. 10:10). David and the Israelites "were celebrating before God with all their might, with song and lyres and harps and tambourines and cymbals and trumpets" (1 Chron. 13:8). No fewer than 120 priests were appointed as trumpeters, with clear instructions "to make themselves heard in unison in praise and thanksgiving to the LORD" (2 Chron. 5:13). This is worth bearing in mind if we come from a church tradition in which the music is quiet and the people even quieter. So are the psalms. "God has gone up with a shout, the LORD with the sound of a trumpet" (Ps. 47:5). "With trumpets and the sound of the horn make a joyful noise before the King, the LORD!" (Ps. 98:6). "Praise him with trumpet sound; praise him with lute and harp!" (Ps. 150:3). Biblical celebration is noisy, as befits the Savior of the world, and it leans heavily on the brass section.

According to Paul, there is a last trumpet. It is sounded at the return of Christ, when the dead are raised and the living are brought into his presence forever (1 Thess. 4:16–17), and when we hear it, all of us will be instantaneously changed from perishable, corruptible, mortal flesh into indestructible, immortal bodies (1 Cor. 15:50–54). The blast of the last trumpet will bring about the fear of God. It will proclaim freedom at last to everyone enslaved in debt or captivity. It will announce a battle which has already turned to triumph, bringing peace. It will herald the arrival of the true King, and the overthrow of the usurper who tried to assassinate him when he was a young boy. And it will cause creation itself to shout in celebration, as death is swallowed up in victory. "Then the seventh angel blew his trumpet, and there were loud voices in heaven, saying, 'The kingdom of the world has become the kingdom of our Lord and of his Christ, and he shall reign forever and ever'" (Rev. 11:15).

POTS

THE POWER OF GOD

We have this treasure in jars of clay, to show that
the surpassing power belongs to God and not to us.
—2 CORINTHIANS 4:7

You are a pot, and so am I. We are many other things—children, priests, kings, temples, image bearers of God—and we may prefer to think of ourselves in those terms most of the time. But we are also earthenware pots. Storage containers. Jars of clay.

It is an image that Scripture uses on a number of occasions to teach a variety of different (although related) things. To start with an obvious one: pots are made. As useful or impressive as they may be, they are nothing without potters. Unless a potter shapes and molds them, they are purposeless lumps of clay, clods of mud, fit to be trodden on and not much else. And this means that any attempt to deny their createdness is, as Isaiah points out several times, sheer idiocy. "Shall the potter be regarded as the clay, that the thing made should say of its maker, 'He did not make me'?" (Isa. 29:16).

This in turn means that the pot and the potter are not on a level playing field. Pots cannot criticize or argue with potters; it is only through the potter's creativity and wisdom that they exist at all. "Woe to him who strives with him who formed him, a pot among earthen pots! Does the clay say to him who forms it, 'What are you making?' or 'Your work has no handles'?" (Isa. 45:9). The prophets make this point on a number of occasions, explaining that it makes no sense for Israel to try to debate with God about (say) the exile, as if they both have valid perspectives to share and God should listen carefully to all their grievances and then acknowledge that there are failures on both sides and that the truth is probably somewhere in the middle. That isn't how any of this works. Pots and potters operate on totally different levels. So if a pot, like Israel, is spoiled in the hands of the potter, and he decides to refashion it into something else, that's up to him, especially if that decision is a response to Israel's sin in the first place (Jer. 18:1–11; Rom. 9:21–23).

Pots are also very ordinary. This would have been obvious to ancient readers, but it is probably obscured for us by the fact that we no longer store things in clay jars, or if we do, it is because they look antique, arty, or creative rather than because they hold things in a cheap and convenient way. In contemporary terms, the equivalent is not those stylish earthen vases containing sticks and fairy lights that you see in the windows of ideal home stores;

it is a cardboard box in an attic or a plastic tub you use to store the leftover rice in the fridge. (This mundane sense of the word is preserved for us in English through terms like *tin-pot*, meaning "unimportant," or *going to pot*, meaning "in decline.") Pots are regular, everyday, ordinary things. They are notable not for what they are in themselves but for what they carry.

And that, for Paul, is a source of tremendous encouragement. "We have this treasure in jars of clay," he explains, "to show that the surpassing power belongs to God and not to us" (2 Cor. 4:7). It sounds disparaging to talk about human beings, bearers of the divine image, as if we were clay jars, plastic tubs, or cardboard boxes. But it is one of the most hope-filled analogies in all of Scripture, because it shows that although we are unimpressive, unexceptional vessels—and if we are honest about ourselves, we know that we are—our lives and ministries are given eternal significance by the surpassing worth of the cargo we carry.

If I stand at the docks this afternoon, watching the cranes lift those huge metal containers from ships onto lorries, I have no idea whether they contain styrofoam or sapphires. I cannot judge their value simply by looking at them from the outside; their worth is entirely determined by their contents. And if they are full of sapphires, they are of incalculable value, even if they look identical to all the other metal containers, and even if (like many of us) they have seen better days and been battered in transit. In the same way, we have extraordinary treasure—in this context, "the light of the knowledge of the glory of God in the face of Jesus Christ" (2 Cor. 4:6)—in ordinary terra-cotta, so that everybody knows where the glory really comes from. My fragile, weather-beaten ordinariness makes the radiance of Christ shine brighter. God stores diamonds in clay pots, and jewels in jars.

Another thing we have in common with clay pots, as Paul notes in this very passage, is our fragility. "We are afflicted in every way, but not crushed; perplexed, but not driven to despair; persecuted, but not forsaken; struck down, but not destroyed; always carrying in the body the death of Jesus, so that the life of Jesus may also be manifested in our bodies" (vv. 8–10). We are vulnerable beings, not just physically but mentally, emotionally, and spiritually. (It is no coincidence that we are described as jars of clay in the book of the Bible that focuses most on the subject of weakness.) The treasure we carry is indestructible, powerful, eternal, and glorious, but the vessels in which we carry it are all too fragile. Recognizing that we are pots may not make us any less likely to smash, but it will make us less surprised when we do and more inclined to trust that God's power will be shown in the process. When we break, he breaks through.

But he heals us too. He takes the ceramic fragments of our lives and reassembles them, like the master potter that he is, into a whole that is more beautiful than it would have been if it had never been damaged. In the traditional Japanese art of *kintsugi*, or "golden joinery," craftsmen use a lacquer to repair broken pottery, which makes the finished product look like it has been lined with gold. In the hands of the potter, the broken and now restored pot becomes more intricate and more valuable than it was before, precisely in and through its weaknesses.[25] God, according to Paul, does the same with us: he takes the very fragility that causes us to break and turns it into an opportunity to display his restorative artistry and saving power. "My grace is sufficient for you, for my power is made perfect in weakness" (2 Cor. 12:9).

This takes us full circle, back to Isaiah. Seen from one

perspective, pots are basic, ordinary, and fragile. But seen from another, they are handcrafted, molded and shaped with consummate care by a potter who delights in them. They are formed, appreciated, even cherished by their maker and given the privilege of carrying invaluable treasure. And it is on that basis that Isaiah cries out for mercy upon Israel. "You have hidden your face from us, and have made us melt in the hand of our iniquities. But now, O LORD, you are our Father; we are the clay, and you are our potter; we are all the work of your hand" (Isa. 64:7–8). You made us, so please save us. May the hands that formed us now fix us.

Containers go through a lot. Before we ever use them, a cardboard box is pulped, a steel container is furnace-blasted, a glass jar is molten and blown, and a clay pot is spun on a wheel. Even after all that, they do not really get to exist for themselves, but only in order to carry something else. Yet in our case that something is more valuable than we can fathom, a weight of glory that makes all our afflictions seem like dust on the scales. And even in those afflictions, as we are molded and spun and broken and remade, we are safe in the powerful hands of the Potter.

26

FRUIT

THE KINDNESS OF GOD

The fruit of the Spirit is love, joy, peace, patience,
kindness, goodness, faithfulness, gentleness, self-
control.

—GALATIANS 5:22-23

There are nine fruits mentioned in the Scriptures, and most of them aren't the ones we naturally think of. Two of them do not seem like fruits at all, since they are not sweet, juicy, tangy, or refreshing. Two of them, though familiar in the modern world, are mentioned only once apiece in the Bible. Three of them, I would guess, would sound a bit exotic to some of us and would be more commonly found in a Middle Eastern cake than in a

Western fruit salad. The remaining two are the ones we would naturally think of as fruits: green, sweet, juicy, and now found across the world both as edible fruits and in soft and alcoholic drinks. Most of the items in my fruit bowl at home—bananas, oranges, lemons—do not get a mention anywhere, though that does not stop them from finding their way onto Christian calendars and fruit of the Spirit tea towels. So how many of the nine can you name? (For the pedantically inclined, almonds and pistachios don't count.)

The fact that God created fruit and scattered it so liberally across the earth tells us a lot about him. Fruit is full of juice, sweetness, abundance, and life—how could the God who created strawberries be anything other than very good?—and Scripture's first chapter is full of it. What are the first living things God creates? "Plants bearing seed according to their kinds and trees bearing fruit with seed in it according to their kinds" (Gen. 1:12 NIV). What is the first command God gives humanity? "Be fruitful and multiply" (v. 28). What is his first gift to us? "I give you every seed-bearing plant on the face of the whole earth and every tree that has fruit with seed in it" (v. 29 NIV). We may associate fruit with the fall of man, but Genesis presents it as the gift of God.

At a general level, fruit is associated with blessing. Over and over again, especially in Genesis, God blesses people by declaring that they will be fruitful, which is to say that they will reproduce themselves, grow, prosper, and bring life and refreshment to the world around them. One of the twelve tribes of Israel is named Ephraim, which means "fruitful." The Messiah, God promises, will be a Branch who will bear fruit (Isa. 11:1). Israel herself, as a nation, is pictured as "a fruitful vineyard" which will "bud and blossom and fill all the world with fruit" (Isa. 27:2, 6 NIV). Jesus promises his disciples that by remaining in him, we will bear lots of fruit, and it will last (John 15:5, 16). As we read Paul's letters, we discover that this happens through the gospel of Christ and the work of the Spirit in us, as we "bear fruit for God" (Rom. 7:4), produce "the fruit of the light . . . in all goodness, righteousness and truth" (Eph. 5:9 NIV), and see the gospel "bearing fruit and growing throughout the whole world" (Col. 1:6 NIV).

Yet God did not make fruit in general; he made specific fruits with a myriad of flavors and colors. Apricots. Blueberries. Damsons. Cherries. My back garden, despite my horticultural incompetence and utter lack of effort, produces greengages, figs, blackberries, apples, and pears, and they all look different and taste different and ripen in different seasons and at different rates. The diversity of fruits God has created is astonishing, and it is not accidental. Each one makes a slightly different contribution to the world, and we can see this even if we stick to the nine that are mentioned in Scripture.

Pomegranates, for instance, are the fruit of love. The most obvious place to see this is in the Song of Solomon, where the imagery is highly erotic (4:3, 13; 6:7, 11; 7:12; 8:2). "If the pomegranates are in bloom—there I will give you my love. . . . I would give you spiced wine to drink, the nectar of my pomegranates" (7:12; 8:2 NIV). But they appear most frequently in the decoration of the tabernacle and the temple. At the front of the house of God in Jerusalem, for instance, were two giant pillars, and at the top of each were "chains like a necklace," festooned with pomegranates (2 Chron. 3:16). As worshipers approached the presence of God, their eyes would be drawn upward, and at the highest point—where we might expect a symbol of power, like a lion, or even a symbol of fear, like a gargoyle—they saw a beautiful necklace covered in the fruit of love. "If the pomegranates are in bloom—there I will give you my love."

Olives are the fruit of joy. Olive oil makes our faces shine (Ps. 104:15). It is sometimes simply referred to as the "oil of gladness" (Ps. 45:7; Isa. 61:3) or "oil of joy" (Ps. 45:7; Isa. 61:3 NIV), ready to be poured on the heads of priests, kings, and Jesus himself. The psalmist celebrates that he is "like a green olive tree in the house of God" (Ps. 52:8) and describes the life of blessing as having children "like olive shoots around your table" (128:3). God promises that he will "put in the wilderness the cedar, the acacia, the myrtle, and the olive" (Isa. 41:19) and that Israel will "rejoice in the LORD and glory in the Holy One of Israel" (v. 16 NIV). The noisiest celebration in the entire New Testament, as "the whole multitude of [Jesus'] disciples began to rejoice and praise God with a loud voice for all the mighty works that they had seen" (much to the annoyance of the Pharisees), comes as Jesus descends the Mount of Olives (Luke 19:37).

Grapes are the fruit of peace. Vineyards take an inordinately long time to grow, so one of the effects of hostility and frequent invasion upon a country, especially when accompanied by slash-and-burn tactics, is that there are no grapes. By contrast, the coming of the grape harvest is a sign that Israel is living in *shalom*, in peace and harmony with God and her neighbors, with the vineyards fruitful and undisturbed. That is one reason why the prophets picture the future age of peace as one in which the hillsides are covered in vines and flowing with wine, with grapes growing so fast that the farmers cannot keep up with it. "'Behold, the days are coming,' declares the LORD, 'when the plowman shall overtake the reaper and the treader of grapes him who sows the seed; the mountains shall drip sweet wine, and all the hills shall flow with it'" (Amos 9:13). When the heavens and the earth are made new and God's people live in peace and security forever, "they will build houses and dwell in them; they will plant vineyards and eat their fruit" (Isa. 65:21 NIV).

Dates are the reward for patience. We hear more in Scripture about date trees (or palms) than we do about the fruit itself, but whenever we hear about either, the point seems to be that good things come to those who wait. After four hundred years of slavery, a terrifying sea crossing, and a long journey with very little food or water, Israel's first campsite is at Elim, surrounded by twelve springs and seventy date palms (Ex. 15:27).[26] Jericho, the city of date palms (Deut. 34:3), finally falls after a week's worth of marching in circles, waiting for the Lord to bring down the walls. In the Song of Solomon, after seven chapters of romantic poetry, the lover compares his beloved to a palm tree he looks forward to climbing, and her breasts to a cluster of dates; again, good things come to those who wait (Song 7:8). This may be why the two most longed-for events in history—the first and second comings of Jesus—are both celebrated with the waving of palm branches by people who have been patient through tribulation for a very long time (John 12:13; Rev. 7:9).

Figs are the fruit of goodness (and/or badness). In modern English we talk about a rotten apple or a few bad apples in a barrel. In ancient Israel it was not the apple but the fig that was the watchword for ripe, juicy goodness or squishy, rotten badness. Jeremiah 24 uses a basket of figs as a prophetic parable: within Judah there are some very good figs, and God "will watch over them for their good" (v. 6 NIV), alongside some very bad figs, whom he will banish and destroy. Jesus likewise uses figs to point out that good fruit can grow only on good trees, whereas bad trees will inevitably produce the opposite (Luke 6:44), and his younger brother James makes the same point about our speech (James 3:12).

Berries highlight God's faithfulness. Many of the plants in this list require cultivation, or at least planting, to be truly fruitful. Berries grow wild. They are just there, sprouting and sprawling in hedgerows and thickets whether people want them to or not, witnessing to God's reliability and constancy regardless of our efforts. They make only one appearance in Scripture, where they illustrate that when God beats a tree to remove its fruit, there are always some berries left in the branches at the very top (Isa. 17:6). So even when God brings judgment, there is hope that new life is possible, because of the faithfulness of God.

Apples are the fruit of gentleness. In our English translations they appear most frequently when God refers to his people as "the apple of his eye" (Deut. 32:10; see also Ps. 17:8; Zech. 2:8)—the precious, cherished part of the eye which we protect at all costs—although sadly the original Hebrew has nothing to do with apples. But they are also compared to the right words said in the right way at the right time (Prov. 25:11) or to the refreshment that we need when we are sick (Song 2:5) or to the soothing shade and sweet delight we experience in the presence of a lover (v. 3).

Melons and cucumbers impress upon us the need for self-control. Cucumbers appear in the context of warning Judah against exploiting the poor (Isa. 1:8) or worshiping idols (Jer. 10:5). Even more ominously, not long after their escape from Egypt, the Israelites grow bored of the manna that God is miraculously providing and begin to pine for the delicacies and treats of the land where they were enslaved. "We remember the fish we ate in Egypt that cost nothing, the cucumbers, the melons, the leeks, the onions, and the garlic" (Num. 11:5). It is a strange yet strangely frightening complaint. It holds up a mirror to our struggle with sin, exposing the power of fleshly desires—whether for melons, cucumbers, money, sex, or anything else—to distort reality and make people feel as if slavery with melons and cucumbers were better than freedom without them. There is a powerful warning there. Either we practice self-control, or we are controlled by something else.

If you are familiar with Galatians 5, you will have got the idea by now. The fruits of the Word correspond to the fruit of the Spirit.[27] You will probably also have noticed that I have said nothing about kindness, the middle fruit in Paul's list of nine. This was quite deliberate, not because none of the fruits God has made demonstrates his kindness but because all of them do.

Just consider the kindness of a God who creates raspberries. The melt-in-your-mouth softness, the bright-red juice, the tangy sweetness, the way they form a garland on the top of a pavlova—all this from a God who doesn't eat them. Most of the world's fruit doesn't grow in Israel, so even when he took on flesh, God never tasted nectarines or plum cobbler. The delights of peaches, lychees, and guavas were unknown to Jesus or his apostles or indeed to the next few generations of believers. (I sometimes wonder: who was the first disciple of Jesus to taste mango? Did they fall down and worship God when they did?) It would be several centuries before a Christian even saw a pineapple and presumably spluttered with laughter, let alone tasted one. Yet even though neither God nor his chosen people would ever eat them, he scattered fruits like this all over the world for thousands of years, according to their kinds, and according to his kindness.

God brings fruit to the world wherever he goes. So, by his Spirit, do we.

CHAPTER

27

VIRUSES

THE PROBLEM OF GOD

By him all things were created, in heaven and on earth, visible and invisible.

—COLOSSIANS 1:16

I don't tend to see things from the virus's point of view.

With virtually every creature I know about, I have moments when I consider them as living beings in their own right. This is even true of the ones I viscerally dislike: wasps, spiders, stinging nettles, mosquitoes, even cats. I recognize that they have some kind of purpose in their actions, albeit one which frequently conflicts with mine, and that they do the nauseating things they do only because it helps them achieve something important to them. A mosquito bites people in order to get food. A wasp stings because it feels threatened. A cat minces around with a superior look on its face because somebody has to cut human beings down to size, and it might as well be them. If I try, I can see the world, even if only temporarily, from their perspective.

But when it comes to viruses, I find this almost impossible. There are probably good reasons for that. They are invisibly small. They cannot replicate unless they are inside the cells of another creature. I am still not entirely sure I know what they are. But so far as I am concerned, they are a subset of me, or an experience I have, rather than a creature with any agency of their own. When I sneeze, I never ponder the fact that I am helping the virus reproduce itself in other organisms by projecting it several feet away (or, more commonly, that I am foiling its reproductive plans by cupping my hands around my mouth). I never consider that the reason I vomit is because a virus is trying to reach other creatures and/or their water supply, nor that rabies is the result of a particularly fiendish virus that not only infects dogs but then induces them to bite other creatures and so spread itself further. A virus, as I perceive it, is something which happens to me—a bug, a disease, a day off work, even a nationwide lockdown—as opposed to another created entity.

This also means I rarely grasp the drama of the way my body responds to it. When I run a fever, I see it as a symptom of the infection rather than as my body's declaration of war against marauding and unwanted colonists as I unconsciously heat myself up so as to kill them before they kill me. I fail to appreciate the marvel of antibodies, whereby defeating a particular virus once (and this is true of many of the big boys, including smallpox, rubella, measles, and mumps) ensures that I never need fear it again. Meanwhile I tell my children that Calpol will make them better, while having this vague awareness that it will do nothing of the sort but merely make them feel slightly more comfortable while their immune system does the real work of hunting down the offending microbes and showing them who's boss. It's not something I often reflect upon, but every time I get sick, it is war. I want to feel better, which means killing the virus. The virus wants to reproduce, which (if unchecked) could mean killing me. It's a fight to the death, man against microbe, virus versus *vir*, and may the best one win.

If you haven't thought about this much, as I hadn't until recently, you may well find it biologically interesting. But it is also theologically troubling. It means that viruses like smallpox, hepatitis, yellow fever, HIV, and COVID-19, which have killed many millions of people over the centuries, are not merely diseases, infections, or people becoming sick and dying. They are creatures, made and sustained by Almighty God, who knows that they will kill millions of people (let alone animals) and creates them anyway. There are somewhere around 1×10^{31} of them on earth today—if you laid them end to end, they would stretch for one hundred million light-years—and many of them make people's lives miserable.[28] One of them, at the time of writing, has brought much of the world to a standstill. Some of them cover children in painful sores and ultimately kill them. Some of them pass from pregnant women to their unborn babies. Yet there they all are, and every last one of them is upheld by the word of God's power. Few things in creation express the problem of evil more sharply than the virus.

Many of our theological defense mechanisms are powerless against it. "Suffering exists because humans have free will," but it is far from obvious why viruses are required for human freedom, and it seems pretty certain that viruses existed before humans anyway. "Suffering exists because there are physical laws, which are necessary for life," but physical laws could presumably exist without smallpox. "Suffering exists to enhance our souls and prepare us for eternity," but viral infections disproportionately afflict the young, poor, and vulnerable, while the ones who (according to Scripture) often need the most soul work, like the rich and powerful, often escape largely unharmed. "God never meant for there to be suffering," but he continues to sustain trillions of viruses every day, and none of them can replicate unless they are inside the cell of another creature. "Suffering is a consequence of our sin," but that's a pretty tough sell when a baby can contract HIV in utero. There aren't many theological objections which resist our usual apologetic medicine as much as this one.

Having said that, the flip side of this is also true. If we can respond appropriately to the problem of viruses, then our response will also serve as an appropriate reply to the problem of evil and suffering more generally. If we know what to do with viruses, we will be immune to all kinds of attack.

So the question is, how could an all-powerful, all-loving God create viruses, which can survive only by afflicting other creatures? (This is true of all predators, of course, but our experience of viruses sharpens the point.) And the answer—although you're not going to like it—can be expressed in three short, frustrating, yet enormously important words: we don't know.

That's the sort of punch line that can get a book thrown across the room. That's probably what I would have done, had I heard it, when I first became a Christian. But after pastoring for fifteen years, reading a lot of church history, preaching sermons and writing books about the problem of evil, and raising a daughter with childhood disintegrative disorder, I genuinely think it's the best, most honest, and most biblical answer to the problem of suffering. It's an answer you find in Eastern Orthodox, Roman Catholic, Anglican, Reformed, and Pentecostal writers.[29] More important, it's also an answer you find in biblical books like Job and Ecclesiastes. Why do people suffer? We just don't know. Why is there evil? No idea. And we're better off admitting that than trying to guess, let alone (like Job's comforters) foisting our guess on our grieving, bereaved, boil-infested friends.

This is not to deny that Scripture gives plenty of resources to help us. It identifies the two fundamental aspects of evil— sin and death—and shows us both their beginning and their end. It insists repeatedly and stubbornly that the world will not always be like this. It debunks easy answers—especially religious ones!—and narrows the field until we have no option but to hope in Christ. It centers on a gospel in which God conquers both sin and death in the crucifixion and resurrection of his Son. It tells us numerous stories of people who suffered far more than we have yet clung to God nonetheless. It ends with a vision of a world in which all evil has gone. But for all that, it never gives us a direct answer to our most pressing and disturbing question, and it occasionally scolds those who ask for one.

Nor is it to deny that we can find morally satisfying reasons for some suffering. Human choices, physical laws, the enhancement of our souls, the consequences of sin: these can all explain some of the pain we experience, some of the time. But none of them can account for all of it, all of the time. No matter how long I think about it, and no matter how many times my children ask me, I simply cannot think of a good reason why God would create the coronavirus, and in all likelihood I never will. And that's okay.

But that doesn't mean there is no such reason. If God is all-knowing and I am not, there are all sorts of things I would expect God to know and to do that I cannot understand. It is simply to say that I am ignorant of what that reason is. Living with that ignorance can be unsettling and sometimes deeply troubling, especially when suffering strikes us personally. But questions, paradoxes, and mysteries are part of the fabric of Christianity. There is a limit to how far creatures can understand the Creator. Ignorance is built in.

And faith involves acknowledging that ignorance, trusting God in our confusion, and finding hope in the fact that one day "he will wipe away every tear from their eyes, and death shall be no more, neither shall there be mourning, nor crying, nor pain anymore, for the former things have passed away" (Rev. 21:4).

CHAPTER

28

CITIES

THE KINGDOM OF GOD

*Here we have no lasting city, but we seek the city
that is to come.*

—HEBREWS 13:14

Hidden away in the middle of Isaiah, surrounded by judgment oracles that modern Christians find difficult to read, is a tale of two cities.

One is desolate. It is eerily empty, like in a postapocalyptic movie. The people who remain are described as languishing, withered, and scorched. Dust blows down the ruined streets; the buildings are boarded up and tumbledown, and "the wasted city is broken down; every house is shut up so that none can enter"

(Isa. 24:10). Music and laughter have been replaced by mourning and sighing. There is no wine, song, or any sign of happiness whatsoever. "All joy has grown dark; the gladness of the earth is banished. Desolation is left in the city; the gates are battered into ruins" (vv. 11–12). It is the stuff of nightmares.

The other is glorious. In this one, God himself acts as the city walls, ensuring that the poor have a stronghold to protect them and that the needy have "a shelter from the storm and a shade from the heat" (25:4). This city is filled with songs of rejoicing: "We have a strong city; he sets up salvation as walls and bulwarks" (26:1). In contrast to the sealed and boarded-up buildings of the wasted city, the gates of the strong city are always open so that the righteous can wander into it at leisure. Isolation and loneliness have become community and celebration. Wine and music are back, along with a banquet that can only be imagined. Tears and shame have been wiped away. Death and desolation have given way to resurrection life. In contrast to the ruined city, which was withered and fruitless, the strong city is compared to a beautiful vineyard which will first blossom and then "fill the whole world with fruit" (27:6). The worst of times has become the best of times.

You can see why cities have so often been used to picture the contrast between worship and idolatry, between serving the God who made you and being served by the gods whom you made. (Augustine, the greatest philosopher-theologian in history, wrote his largest work contrasting the city of man with the city of God, and John Bunyan's *The Pilgrim's Progress* does the same thing in the form of a story.) Cities are to cultures what espresso is to Americano. Simply by clustering a large number of people in one place, cities both condense human society and exaggerate it, making its vices and its virtues far easier to see. The strengths of a civilization—its artistic, intellectual, cultural, social, and military achievements—are almost certain to be clustered in cities. Then again, so are its weaknesses, divisions, injustices, and sins.

I am writing this in a café in London, and it's the kind of café where they sell vegan cocoa and oat milk and everything comes with tahini (whatever that is) or smashed avocado. There are tables spilling out onto the streets, which are lined with flower sellers and organic butchers and craft beer shops and restaurants where (again) everything is served with tahini or smashed avocado. There is a vast urban park two minutes' walk away and a stunning private housing estate even nearer than that. The whole area feels spacious, leafy, prestigious, and rich.

But if you walk a few hundred yards from here, you quickly find yourself surrounded by social deprivation and inadequate housing. You notice substance abuse and homelessness. Trash has not been removed. Graffiti replaces flowers. People work three jobs to get the equivalent of one good salary, rather than one job to get the equivalent of three. And then if you keep walking for another few hundred yards, you reappear in another gentrified area surrounded by more cafés serving tahini or smashed avocado. In London, this strange juxtaposition feels so familiar that it doesn't shock me anymore, but when I see the same phenomenon elsewhere—in Cape Town, or Washington, D.C., or Istanbul—it often catches me off guard. Cities, like humans, are a puzzling blend of creativity, brutality, selfishness, selflessness, wealth, poverty, hope, and despair. A city presents a society with its own unpainted face, and the portrait is not always welcome.

Nowhere in literature is this point made more vividly than in the Scriptures. Isaiah 24–27, with its desolate city and its strong city, is just one of numerous examples. Genesis compares Babel and Bethel: a city where earth tried to reach heaven with a tower, and a city where heaven came down to earth with a ladder. Most of the cities in Genesis represent rebellion against God—Enoch, Babel, Sodom, Shechem—but they are contrasted with the city with foundations that Abraham looked forward to, whose architect is not a human tyrant on an ego trip but God himself (Heb. 11:10). The classic tale of two cities is that of Jerusalem versus Babylon: the dwelling place of God and the joy of the whole earth versus the center of idolatry, immorality, injustice, and imperialism. (It's worth noting that Revelation 18 presents Babylon as a place of trade, wealth, and worldly power, not poverty and deprivation, so its modern equivalents would almost certainly be selling tahini and smashed avocado. The apostles and prophets are not as genteel as we might want them to be.)

Yet the fundamental urban contrast in Scripture is not between one earthly city and another but between all earthly cities, whether past, present, or future, and the heavenly city that is to come. One of the most astonishing things that Jesus ever said, from the perspective of a first-century Jew, was that Jerusalem was going to face the same fate as that of other imperial cities: it would be invaded and destroyed and judged for its evil deeds (Matt. 23:37–24:28). Forty years after he said that, this is exactly what happened. The Romans razed the temple and set it on fire, and Jerusalem went the way of Babylon, Nineveh, and Tyre. No city built with human hands, not even the city of David, could put the glory of God on full display.

All cities center on something. In the ancient world the center was usually a temple of the local god. In the modern world the gods are still there, but the temples have changed their

appearance; they now look like skyscrapers, government buildings, billboards, or public squares. In some cities the local deity
is instantly identifiable, as in Mecca, Moscow, or Manhattan.
In others it is more ambiguous: my city centers on Ares, god of
war (from Westminster to Trafalgar Square), Eros, god of sex
(from Piccadilly Circus through Soho), and Mammon, god of
possessions (from Bank to Bishopsgate). Wherever you go, the
urban god(s) reflect the highest good of the city, which in turn
reflects the highest good of the civilization. But there is no city
on earth—not Jerusalem, Constantinople, or Rome—that is une-
quivocally devoted to worshiping the true God, and him alone.

Yet.

There will be, though. The apostles were clear about that.
There is a city that Abraham looked for, whose designer and
builder is God (Heb. 11:10). There is a Jerusalem above, who
is free, and she is our mother (Gal. 4:26). There is a heavenly
Jerusalem, the city of the living God, filled with worshiping
angels and the assembly of the firstborn (Heb. 12:22–23). There
is a new Jerusalem, a city coming down out of heaven from God,
like a bride beautifully dressed for her husband (Rev. 21:2). Her
gates are made of pearls, her walls of precious stones, her streets
are made of pure gold, like glass, and she has a crystal river
flowing from the throne of God and the Lamb. Nothing unclean
ever enters her, and her gates are open the whole time. She is an
enormous cube, twelve thousand stadia each way, half the size of
the United States and reaching to 280 times the height of Mount
Everest. And she is so thoroughly indwelt by the living God that
she does not have a temple; she is a temple (Rev. 21:9–22:5).

In new Jerusalem all of the evil features of your city and
mine are removed. All of their good features—Sultanahmet,

Table Mountain, the Piazza San Pietro, Chinatown, the Louvre, Central Park—are amplified. She is full of art without idolatry, abundance without greed, and peace without injustice. There is music, wine, laughter, and street food. Old people sit in their porches at dusk, and boys and girls play in the streets (Zech. 8:4–5). And best of all, she is centered not on an urban park or monument or skyscraper, nor even on a cathedral or temple, but on a throne. God is in the midst of her, and she shall never be moved.

We look for the city that is to come.

LIGHT

THE BRILLIANCE OF GOD

God is light, and in him is no darkness at all.
—1 JOHN 1:5

It is a bright, cold day in February, and the sun has been up for two hours. In front of me are a row of bare trees that look almost golden in the sunshine. Behind them the winter sky is duck egg blue. The grass is a rich green but liberally scattered with orange and brown leaves which have been there since November. In front of the tree line there is a little pond, its colors changing every few seconds, and the magpies drinking from it have feathers of intense blacks and whites, like a chessboard. To my left is a large, grayish cloud which is glistening in a way that would be ominous if it weren't moving away from me. As I look over my shoulder, there are pigeons on the ground, busily rummaging through the undergrowth; they are gray too, but in a much deeper, bolder sort of way, and sprinkled with dots of blue, sea green, and purple. And behind me, due east, is the source of all this brightness, its strength increasing every minute. I have to shield my eyes from looking straight at it—the sun is still low in the sky—but to the extent that I can, it looks almost white.

Light is so commonplace that I can forget how astonishing it is. In one sense I cannot see it at all: I can see birds and ponds, trees and clouds, purples and oranges, but light itself is not something I can look at. Even when I look at a source of light—a bulb or a fire—what I can see is not the light but the brightly colored filament or flame. There is a sense in which light, as bizarre as it sounds, is invisible.

Yet in another sense I cannot see anything *except* light. Without being illuminated, objects are not visible to me, let alone colors. Put me inside a dark cupboard, and no matter how fierce the blues and yellows of the parrots parading in front of me, all I will see is black. Light, though in some ways invisible in itself, is the source of all visibility.

There is something deeply mysterious here, as there is with the God whose first words—and I don't think this is a coincidence—were, "Let there be light." Everything that has ever been seen was created by one who has never been seen. "I believe in God," begins the Nicene Creed, "Father Almighty, maker of heaven and earth, and of all things visible and invisible." It is only because God created the world that there is anything to see, and only because God created light that there is any way of seeing it. Yet when we turn to look at the source of all this brightness, we are blinded by his brilliance and unable to look at him. Paul, one of the few people in history to see the risen Christ (losing his eyesight in the process), was nevertheless clear that you could not see God the Father, "the King of kings and Lord of lords, who alone has immortality, who dwells in unapproachable light, whom no one has ever seen or can see" (1 Tim. 6:15–16).

If we start to think about light for any length of time, the mysteries quickly multiply. Most of the light spectrum is invisible to us, either because its waves are too long (radio waves, microwaves, infrared) or too short (ultraviolet, X-rays, gamma rays). It may just be me, but I cannot get my head around how mobile phone signals and visible light and microwaves and nuclear radiation are all basically the same sort of thing, just in different sizes. More puzzling still, scientists went back and forth for centuries over whether light was a particle (as Newton thought) or a wave (as Maxwell thought) and have now concluded that it is both. Thinking about it for more than a few minutes makes my head spin.

Light, it seems to me, is like time: I know what it is until someone asks me, at which point I have absolutely no idea.[30] It is paradoxical, intangible, and essential. Manifold yet one. Kind of everywhere and kind of nowhere. Illuminating everything but illuminated by nothing. Foundational for life, knowledge, beauty, and human experience, while at the same time indescribable, ineffable, and incomprehensible. Bamboozling to an expert but—praise God!—obvious to a child.

Darkness, by contrast, has no existence of its own. It is not a thing; it is the absence of a thing, which instantly vanishes on the arrival of light. Consider the darkest place you can imagine: in a cave several hundred feet underground, inside a chest of drawers, at the far end of a black slipper. Now imagine introducing the faintest possible light source: a glowworm, an ember, the screen of an old mobile phone. Which wins, the darkness or the light? To ask the question is to answer it. The deepest darkness is powerless against even the faintest light.

Incidentally, I find this a helpful way of thinking about the goodness of God and the problem of evil. We sometimes talk as if good and evil were opposites, with good pulling one way in a cosmic tug-of-war and evil pulling the other way, and the little flag in the middle moving left and right. But the difference between good and evil is not a back-and-forth struggle between competing opposites. It is more like the difference between light and darkness or between being and nothingness. Evil has no existence of its own, any more than darkness does; it is merely the absence of something good, like a shadow or a hole in your sock. So when the light of God's goodness shines, there is no negotiation, no tug-of-war or struggle, with the powers of darkness. Evil flees. Falsehood is driven out by the light of truth. Death is banished by the light of life.

God is pure, brilliant, eternal, uncreated light, and in him is no darkness at all. This is why the story of the cosmos begins with the word of God piercing the gloom: "Lights!" It is why we find God rescuing his people, time and again, by being a light in the darkness: sending a fiery torch at night for Abraham, making the sun stand still for Joshua, giving Gideon victory with three hundred lamps, leading Israel out of Egypt in a pillar of fire, and destroying their enemies as the sun rises the next morning.

It is why those who look to God have radiant faces (Ps. 34:5). It is why Jesus, transfigured before the disciples, has a face that shines like the midday sun, and clothes which are as white as light. It is why angels, the messengers of God, are dazzling too. It is why the sun itself will be redundant in the new creation, because the new creation will be lit by the glory of God and the radiance of the Lamb (Rev. 21:23). It is why Jesus said that he is the light of the world (John 8:12) and then promised that his followers would be as well, so we had better get out from under the bed and start illuminating the world with our fiery lamps (Matt. 5:14–16). It is why Isaiah, anticipating the birth of Jesus, predicted that the people who walk in darkness would see a great light (Isa. 9:2) and why Simeon, holding a newborn baby in his decrepit old hands, rejoiced that the light was now here so he could die happily (Luke 2:29–32). "The true light, which gives light to everyone, was coming into the world" (John 1:9).

There is a flip side to all this. The psalmists cry out from the darkness, weeping into their pillows at night. Darkness is the time of secrecy, drunkenness, immorality, and wrath, which means that Christians need to be vigilant and awake (Eph. 5:8–14). Judgment comes like a thief in the night. The angel of death strikes at midnight. The Assyrian army is destroyed at night. So are the people of Sodom. So are the Midianites. Every time we share the Lord's Supper, we remember the night Jesus was betrayed, and at the moment Judas leaves, we get one of the darkest lines in any of the gospels: "And it was night" (John 13:30). All of which means that when we hear the howl of desolation from the cross—"My God, my God, why have you forsaken me?" (Matt. 27:46)—and see that the sky has turned black at midday for three hours, we understand. We recognize the cosmic horror of what is happening as all of our darkness, our perversions and nightmares, our secrets and lies, crowd in upon the Light of the World like a demonic horde, until at 3:00 p.m., with a final cry, the light goes out. No night is bleaker than the night of death. No place on earth is darker than a cave with a stone rolled across the entrance.

But it also means that when we see a group of women walking east in the gloom on Sunday morning, and then the sun beginning to emerge beyond the horizon, waking up the birds and casting a faint yellowish glow across the scrubland, we can make a good guess as to what will happen next. "In him was life, and the life was the light of men. The light shines in the darkness, and the darkness has not overcome it" (John 1:4–5).

Brilliant.

CLOTHES

THE REVELATION OF GOD

*Then I turned to see the voice that was speaking
to me, and on turning I saw seven golden
lampstands, and in the midst of the lampstands
one like a son of man, clothed with a long robe
and with a golden sash around his chest.*

—REVELATION 1:12-13

Storytellers know that dramatic events, particularly those with lots of characters, can be hard to follow. So to help their audiences make sense of the plot, they often give the main characters symbolic clues to their identity. In cartoons the villains scowl and speak with gravelly or breathy voices, and the heroes smile and sound all-American. In movies a menacing bassline in the minor key announces the arrival of a dangerous person, while comic figures appear with bouncier melodies. In plays the symbolic clue might be a costume. In epic poems it might be an adjective ("swift-footed Achilles"). In children's books it is often physical features; the baddies in the Enid Blyton books I read as a child always seemed to have thin lips and cold blue eyes.

In the Scriptures you can often tell a lot about the characters by looking at their clothes. That may sound strange, but if you pause for a moment, you will probably be able to think of examples. Joseph and his coat of many colors. His father Jacob tricking his brother Esau out of his blessing in a game of dressing up. The priests in the tabernacle with their meticulously prescribed garments of gold, blue, purple, and scarlet. King Solomon in all his splendor. The lovers in the Song of Solomon. John the Baptist dressed in camel hair and a leather belt, revealing that he is the new Elijah, the wild prophet who will confront the wicked king and anoint a new one. Clothes reveal characters.

Nowhere is it clearer, however, than in the books of 1 and 2 Samuel. When we meet Goliath, he is covered from head to foot in scaly armor, which makes him sound like a serpent or even a dragon, so when we find the snakelike accuser lying dead, his head crushed by the anointed king, we are not especially surprised. When we meet Samuel, he is described as "a boy clothed with a linen ephod" (1 Sam. 2:18). Straightaway, we know that he will function a bit like a priest.

Right after this we hear that "his mother used to make for him a little robe and take it to him each year" (v. 19). Samuel's robe will come to represent his prophetic authority throughout the book and form a major part of the plot. It is this that Saul rips, accidentally symbolizing that his kingdom will be ripped away from him and given to David (15:27–8). It even features after Samuel has died. When the medium of Endor raises Samuel, on Saul's request, Saul knows who it is because he is "wrapped in a robe" (28:14).

Saul likewise has a robe which comes to symbolize his royal authority (or lack of it). In one of the story's most dramatic moments, David refuses to kill Saul while he is going to the bathroom, but instead cuts off a corner of his robe (24:4–5). At face value this is an act of kindness, as David spares the man who is trying to kill him. But as readers, we know there is more going on. Saul's kingdom will indeed be cut off and given to David, and it won't stop there. Eventually the entire nation will be torn, like a garment, into twelve pieces (1 Kings 11:30–32).

Some of the symbolism is more ambiguous. When Jonathan removes his outerwear and armor and gives it to David (1 Sam. 18:4), we know that he is relinquishing more than his clothes; he is taking his very status as heir to the throne and giving it to his friend. But this makes us wonder: is the same thing happening in that famous scene where Saul makes David try on his armor? The kids' Bibles make this a story about a child trying on clothes that are too big for him, but the story suggests some other contrasts. Saul uses the same weapons that the Philistine champion uses, whereas David uses totally different ones. Saul looks like the kings of the nations; David looks like a shepherd. Saul has divested himself of royalty, without realizing it, and given it to David (even though it will be fifteen chapters before the kingdom changes hands). David, for his part, has refused Saul's way of doing things and chosen to fight in the name of the Lord of Hosts instead.

Then there are those strange moments when kings take off their clothes. Saul strips naked while prophesying and remains unclothed all day and all night (19:24), as if to demonstrate that he has gone mad and has been abandoned by God. Later he removes his royal garb and, like King Lear, disguises himself as someone else (28:8). With his prophetic anointing and kingly power gone, we know it is only a matter of time before he loses his life. When he does and the news reaches David, we can tell what is coming; the messenger arrives "with his clothes torn and dirt on his head" (2 Sam. 1:2).

All of these protagonists take part in a dress rehearsal for another king of Israel, who will combine the robe of a prophet, the ephod of a priest, and the armor of a king. Jesus, like Samuel, will have clothes that represent divine authority, and even the power to heal incurable diseases (Matt. 14:35–36). Like Jonathan, he will take off his outerwear in order to equip, serve, and even wash the feet of his friends (John 13:3–4). Like David, he will be farcically dressed to look like the kings of the nations before going out to fight alone, unclothed and unarmed, as a shepherd. Like Saul, he will be stripped naked, as if to demonstrate abandonment by God, and die in the battle against the enemy. But on the third day he will rise, leaving a neatly folded pile of clothes behind him. When we next hear about his wardrobe, he is "clothed with a long robe and with a golden sash around his chest" (Rev. 1:13).

Intriguingly, his robe on that day is never described as white. Many of us imagine Jesus returning in white garments, because it seems like the sort of color that the triumphant Son of God might wear. But Revelation doesn't say that. Instead it describes Jesus' garments as "dipped in blood," whether that refers to his blood, ours, or that of his enemies (19:13).

At the same time, John insists that the people wearing white robes are actually the church, pure and spotless and stain free, like a bride beautifully dressed for her husband (Rev. 3:5, 18; 6:11; 7:9; 21:2). Our filthy garments have been replaced by fresh ones (Zech. 3:1–5), and in Christ our characters are as clean as our clothes. In a glorious exchange of wardrobes, Jesus' sacrifice has made his robes crimson. But it has made ours white.

> I will greatly rejoice in the LORD;
>> my soul shall exult in my God,
> for he has clothed me with the garments of salvation;
>> he has covered me with the robe of righteousness,
> as a bridegroom decks himself like a priest with a beautiful
>> headdress,
>> and as a bride adorns herself with her jewels.
> —Isaiah 61:10

CONCLUSION

THE GOD OF THINGS

Oh, the depth of the riches and wisdom and knowledge of God! How unsearchable are his judgments and how inscrutable his ways!

"For who has known the mind of the Lord,
*   or who has been his counselor?"*
"Or who has given a gift to him
*   that he might be repaid?"*

For from him and through him and to him are all things. To him be glory forever. Amen.

—ROMANS 11:33–36

CONCLUSION

Today has been ordinary. The sun rose before I did, casting dreamy light across the garden and causing the droplets left over from yesterday's rainfall to glisten on the grass. If the angle is right, little rainbows can be found in some of them. There is a gentle breeze, and occasionally a gust unsettles a flurry of blossom, which floats down and settles on the stones next to the fig tree. Visibility is good, so I can see the hills in the distance. This afternoon we will take the children there for our daily walk: the coronavirus lockdown means we get an hour of exercise per day, and the kids love seeing the sheep with their lambs, the cows with their horns, the fields covered in wildflowers, leading up to Belle Tout Lighthouse, and behind it the sea.

It is currently midmorning. I got dressed and had my toast and coffee early, but my daughter is still in bed, enjoying the fact that the schools are closed. My sons are making a smoothie—berries, bananas, oats, honey, and almond milk, they tell me—and later they will eat a lunch that will almost certainly involve bread, salami, and a bit of salt. Rachel is picking up dust with a tool, a process that in normal circumstances we call hoovering. It occurs to me that of the thirty things we have looked at in this book, I have already interacted with at least twenty-five of them, even though I have been awake for only a few hours and haven't left my house. The only ones I am pretty sure I will not encounter today are donkeys and earthquakes, and possibly trumpets. (Don't ask.)

We worship a God of things. The cosmos is filled with them: everyday, mundane, quotidian, humdrum, ordinary things. Sometimes they delight, sometimes they exasperate, and sometimes they escape detection altogether, but whether quietly or loudly, they insistently point beyond themselves to the God who made physical stuff. Everything in creation tells us something about our Creator.

Paul, concluding his longest theological argument (Romans 9–11) and his richest doxology (Rom. 11:33–36), marvels that God is the one for whom, through whom, and to whom are all things. All things are for him: they exist on account of his wisdom, as a result of his creative work, and for his glory. All things are through him: they are sustained by the power of his word and held together in his mighty hands. All things are to him: they resound in his praise, forever prompting people to ask what God must be like if he made nebulae, jade, triggerfish, and mushrooms. Paul's intention is mainly to highlight the universality of God's rule and the extent of his wisdom and reassure his readers that if God has done something they don't understand, the problem is at their end rather than his. But in doing so, Paul has given us a wonderful excuse to serve as exegetes of creation, our imaginations marinated in Scripture, mining the things of God to encounter the God of things.

For now, the created order is filled with signposts. "All flesh is grass, and all its beauty is like the flower of the field" (Isa. 40:6). "All my springs are in you" (Ps. 87:7). "You are my lamp, O Lord" (2 Sam. 22:29). "He is like a refiner's fire and like fuller's soap" (Mal. 3:2). "You shall call your walls Salvation, and your gates Praise" (Isa. 60:18). "Your rod and your staff, they comfort me" (Ps. 23:4). One of my dreams in writing this book has been that you, driving to work or breastfeeding a child or taking a lunch break, might look around you and see reasons to worship that you hadn't noticed before.

But the day is coming when the signposts will not be needed, because the reality is here. We will know fully, even as we are fully known. And on that day—the day for which, Paul tells us earlier in this letter, creation itself is groaning in the pains of childbirth (Rom. 8:22)—the things of God will stop pointing and start praising. "The mountains and the hills before you shall break forth into singing, and all the trees of the field shall clap their hands" (Isa. 55:12). "Let the rivers clap their hands; let the hills sing for joy together" (Ps. 98:8). "The stones will cry out" (Luke 19:40 NIV). The things of God will sing to the King of Kings and the God of things, for whom and through whom and to whom they exist.

So will we.

ACKNOWLEDGMENTS

Whenever I write a book, I get far more help than I deserve. Some of it comes in practical form: books, space, coffee, childcare, the time to read and think. Some of it comes in theological form, as people teach me either what to say or how to say it. Some of it comes through encouragement and prayer, which is where the power really comes from. Thank you in particular to Hannah Anderson, Judith Barnett, Terri Belsey, Matt and Lauren Chandler, Addis Douglas, Martyn and Gaynor Dunsford, Richard and Jenny James, Andy and Janet Johnston, Carl and Caren Jones, Scott Jones, James Jordan, Simon and Annie Knightley, Peter Leithart, the elders and trustees at King's Church London, Ryan Pazdur, Matt Reynolds, Rob Tervet, Steve and Deb Tibbert, everyone at Urban Ground, Charles and Julia Wilson, and Erik Wolgemuth. And most of all, thank you to Rachel, who has spent fifteen years loving, teaching, encouraging, working with, and praying for me and making me laugh. He who finds a wife finds a good thing.

NOTES

1. Jonathan Edwards, *The End for Which God Created the World*, 1:4.
2. Augustine, *De Doctrina Christiana* 1.3–4.
3. C. S. Lewis, *Letters to Malcolm: Chiefly on Prayer* (New York: Harcourt, 1963), chap. 17.
4. See Eugene Peterson, *Christ Plays in Ten Thousand Places: A Conversation in Spiritual Theology* (Grand Rapids: Eerdmans, 2005), 76: "This is the Genesis origin of who we are: dust—dust that the Lord God used to make us a human being. If we cultivate a lively sense of our origin and nurture a sense of continuity with it, who knows, we may also acquire humility."
5. One possible explanation is that animals which break the normal order of things are seen as symbols of chaos and hence death.
6. I owe this wonderful phrase to Francis Spufford, *Unapologetic* (London: Faber and Faber, 2012), 115.
7. It is interesting that the first miracle God does after Israel has crossed the Red Sea and left Egypt behind is to heal bitter water by sweetening it (Ex. 15:22–25).
8. Naomi Wolf, "The Porn Myth," *New York* (May 24, 2004), https://nymag.com/nymetro/news/trends/n_9437/.
9. Zechariah 14:4; Acts 1:11.
10. My first book, *Deluded by Dawkins* (Eastbourne: Kingsway, 2006), identified sixty-three lines of argument in *The God*

Delusion, of which only eight provided substantial reasons to disbelieve in God (although with hindsight I may have been a bit generous here). Much of Dawkins's book consisted of arguments which were either obviously or trivially true.

11. Of the numerous critical reviews of the book, the best (and arguably the most excoriating) came from Terry Eagleton in the *London Review of Books* (October 19, 2006).

12. Sally Lloyd-Jones, *The Jesus Storybook Bible* (Grand Rapids: Zondervan, 2007), 47.

13. We look further at this idea in the chapter on viruses.

14. Although in some ways not really, as the next three paragraphs explain.

15. See Scott Swain, "God Clothed in Metaphor" (November 1, 2019), *www.scottrswain.com/2019/11/01/god-clothed-in-metaphor-the-lord-god-is-a-sun-ps-8411/*.

16. Having said that, I should point out that the salt familiar to Jesus' audience would probably not have been pure sodium chloride but a mixture of sodium chloride, magnesium chloride, potassium chloride, calcium sulfate, and other impurities.

17. Peter Leithart, "Salt of the Earth," *First Things* (January 16, 2015), https://www.firstthings.com/web-exclusives/2015/01/salt-of-the-earth.

18. There are a number of indications in the passage that Mark is highlighting Jesus' divinity here, and in particular the parallels between Mark 6:48 and Exodus 33:22; Psalm 77:19; Isaiah 43:16; Job 9:4–11 (LXX). See Richard Hays, *Echoes of Scripture in the Gospels* (Waco: Baylor Univ. Press, 2016), 71–73.

19. Augustine, *Confessions* 1.

20. Theologian Kathryn Tanner calls this relationship "non-contrastive transcendence" (*God and Creation in Christian Theology: Tyranny or Empowerment* [Minneapolis: Fortress, 1988]); it is also often referred to as "compatibilism," based on the claim that divine and human agency are compatible with one another.

21. There are a tiny number of elements which expand as solids (silicon, plutonium, and a handful of others), but none which is a liquid in its natural state.
22. This is one of many such connections made in Malcolm Gladwell, *Outliers: The Story of Success* (London: Penguin, 2009).
23. Sam Allberry, *Seven Myths about Singleness* (Wheaton: Crossway, 2019), 142.
24. James Cone, *The Cross and the Lynching Tree* (Maryknoll: Orbis, 2013).
25. I owe this point to Glenn Packiam, *Blessed, Broken, Given: How Your Story Becomes Sacred in the Hands of Jesus* (New York: Multnomah, 2019), 92.
26. The combination of twelve and seventy here is also significant. There are twelve tribes of Israel and seventy gentile nations (Genesis 10), twelve springs and seventy date palms, twelve apostles and seventy disciples sent out on mission (Matthew 10; Luke 10). As such, the palm (Hebrew *tamar*) may also represent gentiles, like Tamar in Genesis 38, and the massive, multiethnic, palm-waving multitude of Revelation 7.
27. I should probably clarify that I don't think Paul, or anyone else in Scripture, was trying to make this connection in an explicit or exclusive way. That said, I think the parallels hold up quite well.
28. "Microbiology by Numbers," *Nature Reviews Microbiology* 9 (2011): 628.
29. Books which deal with this particularly well or thoroughly include David Bentley Hart, *The Doors of the Sea*; C. S. Lewis, *The Problem of Pain*; Fleming Rutledge, *The Crucifixion*; Alvin Plantinga, *God, Freedom and Evil*; Tim Keller, *Walking with God through Pain and Suffering*; and perhaps most powerfully, Fyodor Dostoevsky, *The Brothers Karamazov*.
30. Augustine, *Confessions* 11.